Information Security for Realists

Getting Started with Your Eyes Wide Open

Warning: This book may contain opinions on information security concepts and issues which are held by the author and practically no one else.

Table of Contents

Introduction

"Ransomware is more about manipulating vulnerabilities in human psychology than the adversary's technological sophistication." – James Scott

Has This Ever Happened to You?

Just a few years ago, I had an older, but very useful computer on my desk. It was loaded with applications, code, important invoices and other documents, and life was good. It was a Windows computer, running Windows 7. Or Windows 8? Windows 10? No matter. It's all Windows, right?

I had seen some kind of popup or warning a while back, saying that a patch could not be applied or something, but so what. Nothing lately.

Then the inevitable happened – WannaCry and Ransomware. My computer was now a paperweight. As Homer Simpson once pointed out, a paperweight is nice, but a computer is better.

I was certainly not going to pay the ransom (What's a Bitcoin anyway?) so I replaced the computer about an hour later. Back to work, after checking the Operating System number on the new machine, which was running Windows 10. Full speed ahead!

I was able to recover quickly because I had taken lots of backups on a regular basis (more on that later). They weren't automated, but I did them manually often enough. And I had used a Gmail account to email myself the really important files whenever they were changed or created. So that was basically an extra set of backups.

My coworker had a similar incident a year earlier, but he was an avid user of Google Docs and Google Sheets, and so he had backups available too. All at zero cost and little effort.

Lesson learned – and not just keeping your computer patched and updated. We had used free or low-cost options to keep backups and minimize the effect of a successful ransomware attack. The attack was successful, but not devastating.

There are many fantastic, complex, expensive security tools and strategies available for the big players. However, doing things to protect yourself and reduce your risks can be easy – and that's the point.

A Bit About Me

I have a degree in Computer Science, an MBA, and certifications in various security topics, like Security+, Certified Ethical Hacker, and Certified Information Security Management. My experience, over more than three decades, includes software development, project management, project planning, teaching course-development, and managing a small business. My background is broad, but maybe not too deep nor too technical. No, I cannot sit at your computer and hack into your college grades, your social media accounts or your bank balance. I guess I am more of an entrepreneur and manager than a hooded threat to society.

I have seen enough YouTube videos on a variety of technical topics to know that there are lot of talented programmers and security consultants out there who are very sharp. There is a lot of good learning material on the web that's there for the taking. Quality varies, but overall, I am impressed with what's available, most of it for free.

I tend to speak directly and state my opinions, which don't always align with everyone else's views. I am not afraid to disagree with people who know more than I do. I am not afraid to be wrong.

In addition, I have a point of view. I have seen a lot of money thrown at data security in some quarters. Yet for other companies it's too much bother to even generate a few foundation documents and do some minimal training. So, I feel like we all should be on the same page as far as basic concepts, best practices, and simple steps that are really cost-effective. That would be a step forward – understanding what is available and what makes us safer.

My goal is to improve your data security and reduce your chances of suffering a data breach, without disrupting your business. I believe that the simpler, low-cost steps should be implemented before more complex, expensive techniques are considered. The chapter "If You Can Only

Do X Things" is for those with limited budgets and a desire to keep things simple.

This book is dedicated to businesses and organizations why are doing little or nothing about Information Security because it's too darn complicated and expensive. Let's see if we can provide some clarification and maybe a nudge forward.

What We Won't Do Here

"Technology is a word that describes something that doesn't work yet." – Douglas Adams

T ypes of hackers

You may have seen the list of types of threats and the sources of cyber attacks. Labels like "script kiddie" and "organized crime" are examples. We won't dive too deeply into those categories here.

F amous hacks

By now everyone knows about the well-documented data breaches at places like Target and the federal government's Office of Personnel Management. And of course, political targets and opportunities for nation states to attack each other abound. You can get the salacious details elsewhere. Here we will only touch on related concepts (like supply chain access in the Target breach) of a few incidents.

Detailed technical solutions

There are some fantastic products and services in the marketplace, and I have been to many trade shows and conferences where they were on display. You can find powerful, robust software tools of all kinds and they are only getting better as time passes. But here we will only mention a few of the various tools and technologies in passing. You can know that a bit of web searching will turn up a treasure trove of additional product and technical information.

Instead, we'll look at the basics, and ask "Why?" We will keep it simple at all costs – this material is not your ticket to an industry-recognized certification and a career in cybersecurity. (There are books and video courses available that will move you toward industry security certifications, and they are generally very detailed and really good.)

Our conversation here is geared more toward developing a better understanding of what options you have to defend yourself and which ones make sense under most conditions.

Is This In The Right Order?

"We are stuck with technology when what we really want is just stuff that works." – Douglas Adams

You can certainly read the Table of Contents to determine the order of Chapters here. But let's see if we can simplify our approach in a few sentences.

First, there is a broad introduction, including much more than the information under the "Introduction" heading. That's because Information Security is such a broad, and growing, subject area. There are a lot of viewpoints and knowledge tracks, and I want you to know where I am coming from. This is not a technical manual.

Following that are chapters that provide an overview of Info Security, with an effort to keep it simple. Concepts are described which should help you get your arms around the security field, at least partially.

Next, we take time to look at a sample Information Security Policy (ISP), or more accurately a template, since everyone's ISP will be a bit different. This foundation document is at the heart of a good data security program. This ISP template is fairly comprehensive – it's the only detailed sample document or tool in the book.

And yes, we use the terms Information Security, Info Security, Data Security and Cybersecurity more or less interchangeably. They are not really synonyms, though. One distinction would be that Info/Information Security can include paper documents that have nothing to do with "Cyber". We need to secure the information that's on paper, too.

Training is discussed next, mainly because it's so critical. There is no investment with better "bang for the buck" than a good training initiative. There are several types of training, based on the target audience. A training program may utilize face-to-face training, online courses, or a combination of the two.

We lightly cover the use of Artificial Intelligence or "AI" next, even though that's a massive subject that we don't come near to doing justice to. If you work with AI, or with adding AI to data security, you will need to engage in a rigorous program of study. Not to mention a lot of trial and error. But we will look at a couple examples here. AI is not to be feared, in my view. It is there to be admired, understood, and utilized where it makes sense. And yes, it also has to be managed, controlled, and sometimes overridden.

And finally, the Parting Shots chapter contains excerpts from brief articles I have written on various topics. Caution: This section contains the author's opinions!

Making Information Security Easy

"It has become appallingly obvious that our technology has exceeded our humanity." – Albert Einstein

Strategy

This is one of the most widely-used, least-understood terms in the study of … anything. I am convinced that most people have their own definition of strategy, and it does sound good, right? We know strategies are defined at a higher level than tactics, but the two are definitely related.

Suppose a football coach knows he has a weak defense. He may choose a strategy of attempting to score a lot of points, even if means taking risks, in order to overcome the expected high score for the opponent. And his tactics may involve passing rather than running the ball, to score more quickly.

Or maybe your strategy for achieving a high income involves attaining advanced degrees in computer science or business. While your brother may have decided that being a smooth-talking grifter is the best strategy for him.

Rather than grinding out a long, formal definition of what a good Cybersecurity strategy may look like, let's come up with a few simple examples. Each of these is a possible strategy for keeping your critical information safe and avoiding data breaches.

Acquire the best defensive technology you can afford, budget for high-end solutions and professional staff, hire an experienced CISO and have him report directly to the CEO.

Harden your internal network with strong configuration choices, forbid off-site network access and business partner logins, and keep your web site on an external third-party network.

Rely on SAT training and a strong security culture to encourage cyber hygiene and password management, since most cyber incidents are a result of social engineering or phishing anyway.

Rely on regular, heavy pen testing with formal red and blue teaming, and continuous vulnerability scanning in between pen testing projects.

Enlist an outside firm to organize and manage your entire security program, and purchase cyber insurance to cover any losses should an incident occur anyway.

Wishing and hoping (yes, this a common security strategy - it's economical and risky)

We could go on, but you get the idea. What's your information security strategy? You should be able to describe it in an elevator ride.

Visual Cues and Warnings

What color is today's problem?

Let's say you are developing a good, user-friendly security consol. It could be the go-to interface that a CISO relies in to present the best overview of the current data security situation. Or maybe it's just a simple tool that helps an IT staffer look for problems on the network.

Displaying the status of an information asset (computer, server, endpoint or data store) and including the information that the user would like to see can be tricky. Has the software been patched? Are there threats that would target this asset? How critical is the asset or how destructive is the potential threat? Where does my attention need to be focused, and what are the priorities? Which colors are good, and which are bad?

Consider the commonly described "types of hackers". "White hat" means you are on the side of the good guys, and more specifically, you have the owner's consent to try and attack the data or network. If you wear a black hat, you are a cyber attacker with no permission and with bad intentions. And of course, the grey hat would be somewhere in between. Perhaps someone who is trying to find bugs and weaknesses, so they can report them to the company, but does not have permission to do any of this.

What about the types of testing and how they are labelled? "Black box" testing means the attacker knows nothing about the target network or servers. "White box" testing may be done by an internal team who knows everything about the network and it's technology, and has the credentials to probe deep into the data and applications. And true to form, there is "grey-box" testing, which describes a tester who has some, but not all, the knowledge about the systems and data the company uses. This might be an employee who is not an IT professional, but likely is a user of the network, with basic familiarity of features and facilities.

So, the metaphor of color is used to help makes certain concepts easier to understand. Also, various tactics and visual cures have been deployed to help with the design and layout of the consoles or dashboards in use. They generally rely on knowledge the use already has. We already know that red is usually bad, right?

One useful technique is the traffic light system. Critical issues, problems, or messages appear in red, while mid-level issue/threats might be yellow (which does not always show well on a computer screen). Green hints that everything is OK with this item or asset. Sometimes blue is used for tags like "information only".

For skiers, the familiar black, blue and green levels can separate the complex, dangerous (fun!) ski runs from the simple straight, wide, easier path. It works with software systems and interfaces, just as the traffic light system does.

There are also numbered "tiers" for security tools and technology, with or without special colors. Most people have a good understanding of what a tier is already. The first tier should be – in some way – the simplest or easiest tier.

So, what's going on? Installing a TV or a toaster does not require these tactics. If you read between the lines, you are being told that what lies ahead of you can get very complex, very quickly. And things are being simplified as much as they can be, right off the bat.

What's the point? Consider accepting the fact that you can't do everything at once, and maybe you should think about addressing the low-hanging fruit first. Or, if you have limited time, address the high-priority issues now, and delegate or defer the others.

No one has unlimited resources, especially small to medium businesses. So, when a color or tier level indicates a priority or severity, maybe think about handling those items first, and accept that you can't get to every problem. And when color is used to flag the difficulty of a security measure or technology and you have limited security staff, consider doing the simple things first and establishing a track record of success.

Being able to report up the chain that you have corrected/reset/repaired the most critical security issues and you are now working on the lower priority items sounds good, doesn't it?

Different Strokes

Before we make too many more general statements about Info security, let's admit that one size does not even come close to fitting all. Specifically, the industry your company is in, and the size of your company, will change almost everything.

Information and viewpoints included here are intentionally aimed at small or medium companies and organizations, for the most part. And I try and keep everything "industry neutral" as we go along. But let's face it, the importance of information security, and the processes involved, vary widely with your organization's purpose.

Government has its own set of compliance laws and expectations. Healthcare is heavily regulated as far as the protection of personal health data, for one. And a bank, as the reliance on cash and brick-and-mortar sites declines, is almost nothing but a bunch of computers and data. So, regulation of financial institutions is unique and heavy.

On the other hand, if you operate a lawn service on a cash basis, or even a small government department, you might user a lighter touch. Your industry definitely drives your data Security requirements.

Another huge factor is size. If your company has 100 employees, maybe you have 3-5 people in IT. Perhaps one or two of those may be deemed Info Security specialists. And you might hire outside services to leverage your small security team

On the other hand, the company with 10,000 employees would likely have a much larger IT department and a larger security team as well, and a full-time CISO. And they will have plenty of skilled staff to specialize further into various security roles such as Designer or Analyst. Regular penetration testing, using red teams (attackers), blue teams (defenders), and purple teams (follow-up) could be expected.

So, let's never lose sight of the fact that size and industry determine what security measures and controls are feasible.

Secure Behavior – It's About People

Sooner or later, you will hear someone state that "Information Security is a people problem". It really is.

For example, phishing – getting you to click on a link in an email that leads to a bad place – is still a huge problem. There are entire companies whose sole business model consists of working with your user community to prevent phishing attacks from succeeding. They launch fake phishing attacks, track the results, generate user-based "scores" and even single out individual users for additional training. It's a big problem.

And the miscreant with the hooded sweatshirt in the corner of the coffee shop is still there too. But here are a couple of quick non-technical stories from experienced hackers. The first one involves a man with lots of security, network, and military experience.

This particular ("white hat" or "ethical") hacker does not bother with complex exploits or coding. He just carries a backpack full of WiFi routers into a corporate building, and then places them where they will fool people into connecting to them. From there the routers harvest the users' actual network Logins and Passwords, which will provide total access later. He uses badge reader technology to duplicate security badges too, to make physical access and movement a bit easier in some cases.

"I just need to get in the building" he said. I can get in by sharing my cigarettes at the smoking point, giving someone a small pile of cash, or just smiling and following them in the door."

And this one represents many hackers' views: It's the famous question "Why should I spend all day trying to hack into a server and unencrypt your password when I can just ask you for your password and you will give it to me?" It still happens every day.

So, let's consider what is a bare minimum list of behavior guidelines. These tips are for users, and would be a part of any SAT training curriculum.

First of all, don't let people into your building that aren't you. That goes for the guy you just shared a smoke with, the lady with the armload of donuts, and the youngster wearing what looks like the logo of a utility or service company. And especially the person that follows you in though a badge scanner and has no badge.

If you have a Windows desktop computer at your workplace, and you have control of the options and configurations for that computer, do the right thing. Keep your personal firewall turned on – it requires almost no effort on your part. And if you get alerts or messages, or a note from IT, that says there is a "patch" you need to apply, do so. Keep "Automatic Updates" turned on and your computer will handle downloading and applying the latest fixes, including security patches.

Your IT folks may handle this. But they may not handle your laptop or your computer at home, where the same advice applies. Macs and Linux machines have the reputation of being completely resistant to hacking and cyber attacks. This is not really true, although there are differences. So you need to keep these machines current as well.

If you are walking around, naked and unpatched, and/or using an aging version of Windows, you are one step away from a Ransomware attack or data breach.

All the experts tell us to never click on a link in an email, or an attachment. Really? This seems extreme, considering people email each other Word documents, Spreadsheets, and PDF files about a billion times every day. Maybe we can agree that we treat emails from strangers with great skepticism.

There is much more to "Business Email Compromise" than bad links and attachments. Educate yourself on recognizing malicious email messages or take the company training about to be a smart email user.

Also, please don't walk away from your computer at work with it logged in. Anyone who walks by can instantly be you, and they can do a lot of damage quickly.

Secure Behavior is a culture, rather than a strict set of rules. But these will form a good foundation.

Password Management

Yes, it's mainly a people issue as well. We could spend all day and then some on this topic, because it's so important.

There are switches and codes your IT department (or you) can specify in your security settings that impact password management. For example, minimum password length, requirement for small/large/special characters, requirement to change passwords regularly, etc. These help a lot, but other factors are up to you.

Here are some tips:

Don't use a password that's easy to guess. Experts say that passwords like "123456" and "password" are still commonly used. Please.

Don't put your password on a sticky note and display it on or near your computer at work. (If you are working from home don't worry about this one.)

Don't share your password. Technology can't usually stop you, but it's a bad idea.

Do use words in your password. What's easier to remember, "racingclouds#300" or "XfRd4W39M#$". When a super-complex password is used it ends up on a post-it note because it can't be memorized.

The experts say "Don't use the same password for everything. Use a different password for every service, network, site, etc.") Hmmmmm. Does that mean that if you keep passwords for 50 different sites that you have 50 different passwords? Ouch!

Here is another approach, and I know that lots of experienced professionals are using it. Maybe you should keep three passwords that you can use for different levels of required security. One for banking and financial/business sites, and one simpler one for social media, and one for everything else. It's up to you where you use each password, but you get the idea.

Change passwords now and then, even if not required. This helps reduce your risk if your password has been stolen or if you have shared it. (You would never do that, right?) It makes sense as a risk management tactic.

Sorry, I don't do this as often as I should. I like knowing my passwords and I feel like if they are strong passwords they will never be guessed or hacked. So, I may go a year without changing my common important passwords, and several years in the case of passwords for social media and low-risk sites.

Consider a password manager program/app. I said "consider". Some people love them, but I don't use one, for a couple of reasons:

The passwords it generates are generally super-complex and thus cannot be memorized. Ever. They are gobbledygook. So, if you ever wanted to enter one manually because your password manager is not available, that's a problem.

Even worse, what happens if the password manager ever fails? You are going to have a bad day. It can happen.

My VPN company also offers a password manager app, and they advertise it a lot. Well, the VPN I use works great, almost all the time. But last year it did not work properly one day, and even though I rebooted and reset everything repeatedly it ended up costing me $1000 (long story involving sports tickets, but the point is that anything can happen).

Finally, what about two-factor authentication (2FA) or multi-factor authentication (MFA)? These sites usually text you a code, usually only good for a few minutes, that you can use to complete your login. OK, if you are concerned about passwords being shared or being too simple, this can increase security. You will get no argument there.

But it's just too phone centric. It makes several inflexible assumptions about how many mobile devices you have, where you travel, what Wi-Fi is available, whether your phone battery ever dies, etc. Just imagine that you travel a lot and use more than one mobile device. Trying to use a credit card online, you are told that a SMS code is now headed your way. But today you are not carrying the phone that the credit card bank knows about. Oops. Your credit card is now useless and your purchase is not going to happen. (PayPal has come to the rescue in this situation, but only sometimes). And a good hacker can impersonate your phone and grab the texted code as well. It's not a perfect solution.

When there is an email option for the additional login or authorization code to be sent to you, then I am OK with it. But when it's phone-only I don't care for 2FA. It's very popular now, and most professionals disagree with me on this.

A Very High-Level Overview

"Data security is not a singular thing; it's a constant process." – Greg Scott

Several months ago, an education company I was teaming with on a small project had a request for me. He inquired "Can you prepare and deliver a 15-minute overview of exactly what Information Security is"? 15 minutes? Really?

I was a bit frustrated with the idea, but I agreed on the principle that it might be fun to see what pops out of a brief brainstorming effort. And I do mean brainstorming. Soon afterward I put my head down and just started typing. I called it a "40,000 ft Overview" because that's the approximate altitude of a typical airline flight, so it's the highest viewpoint most people have ever experienced in the physical world.

It's included here just in case you ever receive such a request from executive management, and the requestor is too busy to absorb something with more detail. That's about the only value of this item, to be used just in case you are put in this awkward position and need something to start with.

Note: I ran over my 15-minute limit by quite a bit, even using a quick, energetic delivery pace. Talking fast is not the answer.

Information Security – 40,000 ft Overview

Decades ago, "Computer Science" was a single subject. Now it encompasses many subjects and many careers – engineering, programming, administration, etc. The same is happening with "Cyber Security". It's no longer one subject; it's a variety of roles, practices, technologies, and areas of study.

Definition of Information Security (Trimmed down a bit)

The protection of computers, electronic systems, services, and communications, including information contained therein, to ensure its availability, integrity, authentication, confidentiality, and nonrepudiation.

Purpose

Ensuring the Confidentiality, Integrity, and Availability of an organization's data. This is the established CIA "triad" that forms the foundation of Information Security. All types of attacks and defenses can be traced back to one or more of these factors.

Other Names:

InfoSec, Cybersecurity, Cyber Security, Data Security, Information Security

Definition of a Cyber Incident (trimmed)

An occurrence that results in actual or potential jeopardy to the confidentiality, integrity, or availability of an information system that constitutes a violation of security policies or procedures. Data may be stolen, erased, or damaged.

Useful Frameworks

To help practitioners keep track of all the "moving parts", there are widely-accepted "frameworks" available to anyone. They serve as foundations for enhancing and understanding important concepts and defensive measures that help prevent incidents. Best known is the NIST framework in the US (National Institute of Standards and Technology). Also, a framework called ISO 27001 helps a company determine if they are doing the right things as far as security practices, and that they have good documentation.

Cyber Attacks

Most InfoSec incidents are caused by an intentional "cyber attack", which often, but not always, starts with a password being shared, stolen or easily guessed.

The source of an attack could be an employee, a remote hacker, a business competitor, or a nation-state. Many are just mischievous hobbyists, but large, well-funded attackers are becoming more and more dangerous. National and local infrastructure are potential targets now.

The attack target could be a web server, a database server, a desktop computer, your laptop, your tablet, your phone, your refrigerator, or your garage-door opener. Small devices are becoming part of the Internet of Things (IoT). The more connected devices you have the larger your "attack surface".

One common attack that can be devastating is called a Ransomware attack. These are painful and disrupt productivity completely. They essentially turn your computer into a paperweight.

There are complex defenses available to deter Ransomware attacks. But you can reduce the danger (and the damage done) with frequent backups into another computer, and by having your computer automatically apply system updates. This ensures that software fixes for system vulnerabilities are in place as quickly as possible.

Defenses

There are a wide variety of defenses available to an organization which will help reduce the risk of a successful attack. Some are technical, some are administrative, and some are human-oriented, such as training.

A simple list of defenses to get started with may include:

1. Create a Written Information Security Policy
2. Conduct a High-Level Assessment with a Trusted Partner
3. Semi-annual User Security Awareness Training (SAT)

4. Create an Inventory of all your data stores.
5. Use Business Impact Analysis to measure current risk.
6. Create an Incident Response Plan (and Business Continuity Plan)
7. Deploy and configure firewalls.
8. Examine and improve backup policies and procedures.
9. Explore and Consider Automated Security Tools

Everyone has their own list! There are many more cyber defenses that should be considered.

Roles / Careers

There are many roles in the InfoSec world. At the top is a CISO (Chief Information Security Officer) who would often report to the CEO or CTO. Other InfoSec roles include Security Consultant, Security Engineer, Security Analyst, Penetration Tester, and Security Manager. At the Indeed job site, for example, there are many openings in these areas.

Some roles involve "penetration testing" where authorized attackers (red team) try to access protected data, defended by other professionals (blue team) as an elaborate exercise. Companies utilizing red and blue teams typically have larger budgets, while a small company might hire an outside firm and do occasional penetration testing.

Training for InfoSec positions vs SAT

Information Security Training could be somewhat technical and lead to certifications such as Network+, Certified Ethical Hacker, and CISSP. There are many web sites, advanced education programs, and books available to support these areas of study. Certifications would lead to roles such as Security Consultant, Security Engineer, or Security Analyst.

On the other hand, SAT (Security Awareness Training) is intended for all system users and managers within an organization. The focus is usually on better password selection and management, improved security "hygiene", best practices, and why InfoSec is everyone's responsibility. When it comes to "money well spent" it's hard to beat SAT training. In the best case, training is followed by an ongoing awareness campaign that may include wall posters and follow-up training or events. In that case, there may be a "security culture" established, which is very helpful.

Where would we start?

If you are an InfoSec practitioner, you need to align yourself with your company's goals, risk appetite, and culture. Some organizations will just not invest much in better security. Work within the system and be seen as an ally.

You can't do everything at once, and most companies and organizations have limited budgets. Luckily, there is often "low-hanging fruit" to be targeted. These are steps you can take that are not costly or difficult; but are likely to improve your data security.

A POSSIBLE Bare Minimum List (If you can do nothing else)

1. Do a very simple self-assessment, like the one at flex-protection.com.

2. Create a written ISP with strong management support.
3. Create a simple Incident Response Plan
4. Implement and verify automated backups.
5. Conduct SAT training at least annually.
6. Make sure individual computers have Automatic Updates turned on.
7. Turn on firewalls on all computers, deploy a hardware firewall as well.

To Consider and Explore

Someone is trying to attack your computer or company server constantly. Expect that someday they will succeed. Backups and an Incident Response Plan are crucial.

There are many tools and applications on the market, such as intrusion detection / prevention applications (IDFS and IPS), packet sniffer tools, SIEM applications to report consolidated network activity, risk management applications, vulnerability scanners, security consoles, and more. Some are cost-free, and can be downloaded and used on an ordinary Windows, Mac or Unix/Linux computer.

There are many small companies who can help you lay a strong foundation for better security, using template policies and documents and some specific expertise. You can download a flexible foundational Information Security Policy and Best Practices for free at some web sites.

The NIST and ISO 27001 frameworks are free to examine and learn. They have a wealth of information. They are not overly complex so don't be intimidated. Even YouTube is loaded with videos and training materials that will help you prepare for an Information Security certification, or just improve your company's security posture. There is plenty of information on practically every security-related topic out on the internet.

Of course, there is no guarantee the information is accurate, because it's the internet after all. But most blogs, articles, and videos are at least basically accurate and attempt to be honest and informative. Some sources are actually very good.

Concepts To Remember – Streamlined

"Any sufficiently advanced technology is indistinguishable from magic." – Arthur C. Clarke

Here are some concepts that are worth remembering, because you will encounter them again and again. Lots of important details and technologies have been left out in the interest of brevity. Consider this a "starter list".

General

Your Foundation

The foundation of cybersecurity as a science is also known as the "Security Triad" or the "CIA Triad". Like any self-respecting triad, it consists of 3 components:

1. Confidentiality

2. Integrity

3. Availability

Your data, business and personal, should generally be held **confidential**. Unless you decide to share it. And **integrity** just means that someone can't reach your information and modify it without permission. What comes out of one end of a network of process should match what went in. So far so good.

The last goal is **availability**. This one is the most interesting to me. Let's look at availability from a couple different angles.

Imagine that a hacker has attacked your network and erased the database that holds the information you need. That's easy to envision. Or what about a botnet – thousands of enslaved computers working in unison – launching a DDOS (distributed denial of service) attack that clogs your application server so badly that it just can't communicate. That's certainly a violation of the principle of availability.

But consider a computer that has very strict password rules, and you need to log in to get your work done. It forces you to change your password frequently, and it doesn't let you re-use a password you have used before. Now you are racking your memory and trying various password candidates. And your handy post-it note with your latest password scribbled on it was around here somewhere, wasn't it?

This system is definitely unavailable to you. And you are probably a bit frustrated to boot. Maybe you are calling tech support or going through a password reset process. Eventually, you probably will have a new password. And here comes another post-it note.

If you don't think this is a widespread problem, consider that fact that you can shop online and buy a convenient notebook-style "password log" where you can write all your passwords. No kidding. Imagine what kind of pickle you will be in if you ever lose your treasure trove of written-down passwords, or if someone steals that notebook.

Balance

I work in the software field – all kinds of computers and servers involved – and I use a lot of online services (tools, images, editors, etc.). So, it's not unusual to be stuck, at least for a while, as I fumble for a password somewhere. I know you have been there too.

Or maybe imagine that your employee badge does not get you into the data center, where an air-gapped (not connected) computer waits for you in order to get a critical task done. How about logging in and finding you don't have access to a certain folder that you really need?

Is there such a thing as too much security? I think so, but there are people who don't feel the same way. There is a fear factor here. Do you want to be the manager of CISO who weakened security in order to make life easier for users, only to experience a devastating attack later? Maybe erring on the side of being super-strict at all costs is understandable.

This is part of a broader issue, where security personnel are not always perfectly aligned with the company or department, and their goals. I have seen the term "security vs. the business" used to describe it. Ouch! Do users sometimes look at IT and security personnel as adversaries? I think they often do.

The point is, every security measure should consider the users and how they work, and what they need, and how the company depends on their productivity. We're all on the same team, right?

Payback

I have been on the wrong end of a handful of cyber incidents in the last decade. The ransomware attack mentioned above was one. Someone utilizing our company server as a distribution point for illegal videos was another. And a third was a denial-of-service (DOS) attack that was alarming but was of little consequence. (I was also the victim of an identity theft that had nothing to do with computers or technology at all).

Besides the successful attacks, my tech guys have been able to show me server logs that show near-constant attempts to login into accounts that were definitely not intended for public access. I also see attempts to execute "SL Injection" attacks using web pages in our site. Yes, the flow of cyber-attacks and attempts never stops.

I may be a primitive thinker, but I have to admit that whenever I see these things, I get a little angry. I know that on the other end of the attack – be it automated or manual – there is a human acting intentionally. And I would sincerely like to track down that person and punch him right in the nose. How dare they point their technical skills and weapons at my network or desktop computer! I don't even know them. It makes steam come out of my ears.

Unfortunately, it's almost impossible to identify the responsible party and take revenge. It's just too easy to hide using today's internet. The youngster in the hoodie at the coffee shop, and the nation state with persistent threats and advanced technology (I bet you can think of a country, or two) are both pretty well protected.

Further, if you have hacking skills and consider the idea of sending a devastating exploit at the guilty party in return, the law generally frowns on that. The main reason is that you will more likely end up damaging an innocent party than harming the actual culprit. You may wreak havoc on a service provider, a hosting company, or simply the wrong IP number or account. I have read stories of victims pursuing payback, and it does not usually turn out well.

There is an old saying that I like, and it states: "The best revenge is living well." I guess that the corollary here might be "The best revenge is hardening your computers and networks to prevent future attacks from succeeding". That may be a better direction than launching a project to exact revenge. And having a good Incident Response Plan handy would help too!

By the way, the identity theft I mentioned above landed an old friend in prison, and I received restitution for the significant damages. Meanwhile, I have no idea who launched any of the cyber-attacks. This illustrates another lesson: One reason that cybercrime is so attractive to its perpetrators is that the risk of getting caught is much lower than for other types of crime.

Controls

There is one more important concept in the General category. It's really as much as a term as a concept, and the term is "Control". A control is just about anything you do, or write, or implement that has to do with Data Security. You will see the term so frequently in books, web sites, foundation documents and other documentation that you may as well get comfortable with it.

A locked door is a control, a password policy is a control, an encryption program is a control, a backup policy is a control, and so on. Most of the time you can substitute the term "defensive measure" (which is my favorite) for the word "control" and you will be in the ballpark. But lots of standards, documents, and frameworks refer to controls at every turn.

It's not a problem, it's just something to expect. For example, the NIST (National Institute of Standards and Technology) Risk Management Framework, and the ISO 27001 certification standards, feature lists of controls that may be utilized by almost any organization. I feel like the ability to select some controls and leave out others makes these frameworks more flexible and useful.

To take it a step further, the vast ocean of available controls can be divided into three categories:

1. Administrative Controls – rules, policies and other means of guiding human behavior, especially that of employees, customers, and business partners.

2. Operational Controls – manual or automated processes that need to be performed in a certain order and/or in a certain manner. Kind of like instructions, if you will.

3. Technical Controls – technology such as application software, system software, hardware devices, firewalls, packet filters, etc. Strictly speaking, the settings and configuration options that make these devices work in a certain way are controls in this category as well.

Technical

Malware

Consider the threat of malware in general. Yes, malware is still out there. Viruses, worms, and trojans are still proliferating and you still need protection from them. They are often delivered via email, but flash drives and website hacks are used as well. Virus blockers are fairly effective, but they don't catch everything. Lots of info is available on this topic from various online sources.

Ransomware

It has been with us for over a decade now. Devastating attacks, with severe consequences, loss of computer hardware and software, and loss or breach of data. Typically, it makes your computer unusable, but your data can also be stolen and sold, not just encrypted. That means credit card details, financial information, health details, and company secrets can be harvested and sold on the dark web.

The best protections may be:

1. Stay current on patches and fixes.
2. Block email attachments, or only open one if you know the sender.
3. Users can use some training on recognition of malicious emails.
4. Endpoint protection tools, like Bitlocker, can be effective.
5. Software provided by a MSSP as part of its service.

IP Addresses

IP numbers uniquely identify every computer, server, router, or other device on the internet or internal network. These numbers have 4 segments, each with a value between 0 and 255. All web addresses translate to an IP number. Before an address can be useful, a name like MyFavoriteSite.net will be translated into 231.76.43.186 or something like that. There are public and private IP numbers, and the private numbers can only be used on a local network, since the same number can be re-used in other networks. Sometimes multiple web sites actually share a single IP number, so that the limited pool of IP numbers can be used more efficiently.

Malicious actors on the internet change IP numbers frequently, to make themselves harder to track down. Finding individuals who are responsible for hacks, intrusions, data theft, resale, and so on is not an easy task, even when the search stars with a source IP number.

Physical Security

People and businesses have been securing assets since long before computers were invented. So physical security is much older in practice than cybersecurity.

Think of fences, gates, guards, dogs, cameras, bollards, locks, badge scanners, etc.

If you lose the physical security battle, you have lost the war. You will have unauthorized people in your hallways, data center, patch closet – you name it.

Physical security is mainly a people problem. Consider tailgating (entering a building right behind someone who is allowed in via a badge or key), leaving doors open, trusting strangers, and people socializing in the data center where they may not belong.

Encryption

The actual details of how data is encrypted and unencrypted are pretty complicated. They involve encryption algorithms, keys, certificates, and certificate authorities. For now, know that an "https" in your browser location window means that your conversation with the website you are on is being encrypted in both directions, which is good.

As for email, know that Gmail is encrypted using the popular TLS encryption standard between your browser and the Gmail server. And that's great. But if the party you are sending to does not support TLS in their environment, then your email will arrive unencrypted. So it's not an end-to-end solution. A bad actor could still get his hands on your email content.

And be aware that Google runs through all your email and gathers information that will help it advertise to you. That is the sole reason why the folks at Google provide this nice, popular email service. Privacy concerns, anyone?

Encryption is a deep, fascinating subject and there is a ton of information and videos online about exactly how it works in various settings. It is the basic protection for what is called "data in transit" and is also sometimes used to secure data stored on computers ("at rest").

Mobile Devices

Mobile phones can also be hacked. Several attack vectors involve Bluetooth but some don't. IOS and Android both have their vulnerabilities, which are beyond our scope here.

On the plus side, if you are in public and concerned about your transmissions being intercepted, turn off your Wi-Fi on your mobile device and let your phone use the phone service (4G or 5G) for a while. That communication method is well encrypted, while Wi-Fi may not be.

You can also install a VPN on your phone, and it could be (and should be) the same VPN product you use on your laptop. A VPN provides end-to-end encryption. And yes, it also usually fools your streaming service as to what country you are actually sitting in at the moment, so you can watch more movies. But you wouldn't do this, would you?

Log files

Even the Windows firewall on a personal desktop computer can generate copious logs. And a web server will create various log files as well, and they will grow quickly. The truth is that there are often too many logs, logging entries and details for you to keep up with. This is especially true of a larger enterprise with a diverse network.

Fortunately, there are software tools, called SIEM systems, that can automatically combine, filter, and present logged details in a such a way as to provide important details to a security manager.

There are many SIEM options, and they are generally very useful and powerful. If your responsibility includes monitoring server logs, for instance, you need to investigate what SIEM tools are available to make your life easier.

Linux

The Linux operating system has to be mentioned here. The reason is that so many security commands and native tools are part of Linux. The list of Linux commands that retrieve or operate on the data security aspects or a computer or corporate network is lengthy. There are lots of great tools you can use to manage a workstation or network within Linux – it's really amazing.

On the other hand, Linux can be a royal pain for someone who is used to Windows. For one thing, while some GUI (Graphical User Interface) tools and menus are available, most of the time you will be typing into a command line, just like you did in the 1980's.

In addition, Linux is case-sensitive, essentially doubling your chances of creating a typo. A case sensitive operating system (or an application, for that matter) is possibly the most severe insult that can ever be thrown at you. It's really annoying. Yes, that's an opinion and others disagree.

If you plan to be an Info Security professional, you will want to load up your laptop with a special version of Linux that contains all the latest attack/defend applications, security commands and exploit managers. It's called "Kali Linux" and it is your gateway to a strong technical understanding of Information Security tools and details. I put it on my Mac as a second machine, using a Virtual Machine platform, one of several available.

I have to note here that the MacOS (the operating system that a Mac uses) is derived from Unix, as was Linux. So, Mac and Linux OS's have a lot in common. On the other hand, from a technical perspective, Microsoft Windows has little in common with either of these. See notes about "nmap" below.

nmap

One tool that will be part of your knowledge foundation– like a Swiss army knife – is the "nmap" command. It's a native piece of Linux, and that's why it is shown here in small case. Fortunately, there is a very nice Windows version with a decent GUI available. It's called "Zenmap" and it's free to download and use.

There are entire books on nmap and how to use it. Its capabilities are vast and valuable, with lots of parameters that govern its behavior. We can't even scratch the surface here. But here are three things nmap can show you just for typing in a single command:

1. All the machines/devices on your network, or someone else's.

2. What operating system all those devices are running.

3. What ports are open on each of these devices.

4. Much, much, more, too much to list here.

If you decide to build up your skills by practicing your nmap scans, remember this. You can scan other company's networks all day long. But they can see you doing it and know where you are. Further, any kind of nmap scan (and a scan with a vulnerability scanner, which is even worse) can be viewed as a preparation for an attack. The people who manage your target network will probably not appreciate your activity and may even be alarmed. I suggest you scan your own network or get permission.

Management and Design

Risk Management

If you want to get the attention of top management or your board, learn to talk in terms of risk management. That's what they care about, more than technical details.

Entire books have been written on this subject, and rightly so. At a high level, risk management strategies include:

1. Acceptance (live with the risk)

2. Avoidance (stop doing whatever causes the risk)

3. Transfer (buy cyber insurance to cover incident costs)

4. Mitigate (take MEASURES to reduce risk – the most common strategy)

Defensive measures, steps like encrypting data or locking the data center door, reduce risk. Note that a risk is where a THREAT meets a VULNERABILITY. If there is no threat, there is no risk. An unlocked door (a vulnerability) is not a risk if no one wants to come through it or nothing important is behind it.

Further, when risks are countered with defensive measures, the reduced risk that remains is called "residual risk". Add up the residual risks and you have "total risk", which is worth tracking. This is a factor that management MUST be interested in.

At the end of the day, the question management will ask is "How well have you reduced total risk?" This question is aimed at the CISO or security team, more than at network and system users as a whole. BUT as the saying goes, "Security is everyone's responsibility".

To be pro-active, a security team can monitor threats that exist "in the wild" and prepare to defend themselves from them. Numerous threat databases and services exist to allow you to be fed the latest risk details on a frequent basis.

High-end risk management software tools like this available from Qualys will connect with these threat information feeds and include them as part of the detailed picture of your security situation in console form. It's quite impressive, and these tools can be very robust and flexible.

A simpler application like Risk Assistant works with a bit less information. It helps you identify and track security risks, and to associate them with a cost. But more importantly it helps you address those risks with specific measures that reduce the potential damage. In this way, the total risk can be calculated and tracked across time.

Multi-layered Defense

Good cybersecurity is like an onion. And I don't mean it makes you cry sometimes. I mean that when you peel back one layer, there is another layer waiting there. This means a breach in one layer (like sneaking through a gate) would not mean an attack would be successful.

One example group of defenses that are layered would be a security guard, a locked door, and a computer with password protection beyond that. Another set might be a login, a password, 2FA for additional authentication, and then encrypted data on the computer itself.

Attack Surface

This serious-sounding term actually represents a fairly simple concept. The more stuff you have, the more places and the more ways you can be attacked. If you have only two computers and a printer, and they are locked down with most of their TCP/IP ports disabled, and they are not often connected to the internet, you have a very small attack surface.

But if you have your own web servers and email servers, lots of online product information connected to a database, field reps carrying iPads, and a geographically distributed network, you have a large attack surface. In that case, more serious and costly security programs may be called for.

Reducing your attack surface may reduce your risk profile, since you might have fewer vulnerabilities. But wait – you need these devices and interfaces, right? Of course, you want to reduce your attack surface when you can.

Also consider where systems and data are located. Your website requires public access. Should you have your proprietary financial information on the same machine? Not if you can help it.

Consider keeping your web server – if you have one – outside of your main internal network. Establish a "DMZ" for servers and devices that allow external / public access.

Resilience

This is an important concept. Its core question is "How quickly can I recover?"

For a small company with simple operations, it might involve not much more than regular backups, a streamlined Incident Response Plan, and a leader who pays attention to keeping these things current.

For a larger enterprise, there may need to be a "hot site" (a fully-functional workspace to utilize after a disaster to keep the company going). Or perhaps a "cold site" where there is an infrastructure but not much else. Or a "warm site" which is somewhere in between.

So, at a minimum, make sure your critical data and documents are being backed up and know who to call when something goes wrong, which may or may not be an IT person. Expect that your information security protections will fail someday!

Endpoint Protection

Consider all your computers, printers, routers, and other devices as "endpoints". There is a substantial industry comprised of companies who are dedicated to protecting your endpoints for you, for a fee of course. These companies are called MSSP's (Managed Security Service Providers).

I hope we can generalize for a moment. Typically, an MSSP service includes installing a special "software agent" that runs on your endpoints and keeps track of patch status, unusual traffic, and other factors. This software reports back to a console running at the MSSP, where support engineers watch your network for problems. Some of the companies offer an "EPR" service where the "R" stands for response. In other words, they try to handle your issues for you rather than simply report them. This is a high-end option for big companies.

As an alternative, companies like Bitdefender will provide the software and let you do your own monitoring. In essence, you will have your own Network Operations Center (NOC). This is a more economical option, but do you have a technical resource, or a team, who is available 24/7 to monitor everything?

Scanning and Testing

You might consider doing some "vulnerability scanning" on your network, or specifically targeted at your web or application servers. This scanning uses powerful software tools to look for vulnerabilities, based on checklists and software configurations. Make sure the users of the target system know that scanning is going to be done. It may slow the system down and even leave artifacts such as odd-looking data that has been used to test fields and application screens.

There are several great tools available, some for free, to provide vulnerability scanning. Some are designed specifically for web application testing. Make sure you understand what your vulnerability scanning software is going to do before you launch it.

Another piece of advice from security experts is this: If you plan to also do penetration testing ("pen testing"), do lots of vulnerability scanning first, and clean up all the vulnerabilities that you can. Otherwise, if you do pen testing first, it may be a bit too successful, with lots of penetration happening, wreaking havoc on the network.

Cloud Security vs. In-house

"The only truly secure system is one that is powered off, cast in a block of concrete and sealed in a lead-lined room with armed guards." – Gene Spafford

Cloud security? It's a whole new world. The skills, terminology, processes, tools, and concepts that apply in the in-house-network universe don't really apply here. Or more accurately, they apply somewhat, but there are a lot of new concepts to master.

Many companies are currently supporting applications and critical data in both places – on the local network and also on a cloud service. This certainly increases workload and complicates the picture a bit. And that's not all.

If you haven't already done so, jump onto a cloud service (AWS, Azure, etc.) and poke around. See what's offered and what's possible. If you are like me, your first though may be something like "Looks like I have complete control and I can do just about anything". Lots of people have discovered how easy it is to "spin up" a virtual server in the cloud. It's pretty cool for an IT staffer or a technology geek.

Now it's a month later. You are checking your notes. Did I create three servers on AWS last week or one on AWS and two on Azure? Better log in and check. Where did that new one come from?

A company may have one application server in a cloud service, and its employees may have created ten more servers or workstations on their own, for various purposes. Also known as "server sprawl" it leads to an CISO or CIO not knowing where the company's data really lives, and how many machines and data stores have to be protected. That's never good.

This problem (or opportunity) is part of a growing phenomenon called "Shadow IT" and it can quickly get out of hand. The task of maintaining an accurate Information Asset Inventory is made more complicated when this happens.

Don't think that your data is secure just because it's hosted on a cloud service. Cloud Service models include Software as a Service, Platform as a Service and Infrastructure as a Service. You can "rent" anything from a chunk of bare hardware to a fully-configured application server.

What about security? "There is a "responsibility model" with each cloud service that you need to understand. Over-simplified, it boils down to this: The more of the infrastructure you are providing the more you are responsible for security. If you are on "bare metal" and providing the Operating System, Database, and all application systems, you can expect to be responsible for securing your data, as you might expect.

Many companies are currently supporting applications and critical data in both places – on the local network and also on a cloud service. This certainly increases workload and complicates the picture somewhat. Fortunately, there are software tools, often customizable, that help you manage the whole picture. Referred to as "CASB" (Cloud Access Security Brokers) they can show you the whole picture, including multiple cloud providers and even your in-house network. Having your status and threat information all in one console can be very useful.

A basic bullet-point outline might de-mystify the cloud universe just a bit:

Review of Cloud Concepts

- AWS, for example, offers public, private, or mixed public/private (hybrid) OWNERSHIP models. Focus is on public cloud solutions here.
- Three DEPLOYMENT ("as a Service") models are available, depending on the customer needs and capabilities: IaaS, PaaS, and SaaS.
- Infrastructure as a service (IaaS): offers essential compute, storage, and networking resources on demand, on a pay-as-you-go basis (Ex: hardware).
- Platform as a service (PaaS): provides a complete development and deployment environment in the cloud (Ex: Add Operating System and Web server).

- Software as a service (SaaS): allows users to connect to and use cloud-based applications over the Internet. Common examples are email and calendaring.
- Amazon AWS is one choice among many, including Microsoft Azure, Google Cloud, Oracle Cloud, IBM Cloud and others.
- The AWS overall security model is generally pretty clear: they secure the cloud itself, and you secure what's in the cloud.
- HOWEVER, AWS provides many tools and systems to help you secure your systems and data, beyond securing the cloud itself.

AWS High-level Overview (there are other suppliers!)

- AWS is global in nature: it uses many instances (ex: virtual computers) within "Availability Zones", within defined geographic Regions.
- Instances may be your servers, which are also typically virtual and based on templates.
- You can use existing templates or create your own as a basis for creating instances (virtual machines).

- Other virtual devices/components include software firewalls, sub-nets, and routers. You will need to create and configure these.
- You will also need to review the storage options for your data when you create an instance. There are various ways to allocate your storage space.
- AWS has a free tier, with many limitations, as you might expect. A good place to experiment and learn.

Identity and Access Management (IAM)

- IAM is the fundamental information security concept that governs all user accounts, roles, and permissions.
- When you launch your AWS service, you will establish a "root" account, which has total authority and permissions.
- Use the root account to establish user IAM User Groups, and add one or more users to each group. Ex: Administrators, Developers, etc.
- Assign permissions at the group level, and easily add users later. Use the "least privilege" best practice for every user group.

Security tools and benefits provided by AWS

- Most security tools may be activated or disabled as you wish.
- Many existing security strategies that you use on your in-house servers and applications (ex: database table with users & passwords), may be utilized on your AWS virtual machines
- AWS keeps your data safe – AWS infrastructure is robust, with multiple physical and electronic safeguards in place.
- Privacy – your data is stored in secure data centers.
- Compliance Requirements – several compliance programs are provided within the AWS infrastructure.
- Includes attestations, regulations, alignments, frameworks.

Partial List of AWS-Specific Security Features

- AWS Config – compliance auditing, security analysis, resource changes, deployment troubleshooting.

- AWS Service Catalog – organizes resources into Catalogs, including virtual machine (VM) images, servers, software and databases.
- Amazon Guard Duty – threat detection and security monitoring
- AWS WAF – Amazon's configurable Web Application Firewall
- AWS Shield – specific protection from DOS/DDOS (Denial of Service) attacks
- AWS KMS – a key management service useful in managing encryption keys.
- AWS Artifact – tools for compliance management and security reports
- AWS Inspector – designed to access, scan and troubleshoot security issues for applications you have deployed in your AWS account.
- AWS Trusted Advisor – helps improve performance and cost-effectiveness by optimizing your AWS environment.

The other services – like Microsoft's Azure and offerings from IBM and Google, have similar constructs and tools. They are robust, powerful technologies that allow scaling and management in ways that were unheard of ten years ago.

These behemoths have given their cloud security components some serious thought. This isn't something they just threw together.

And there are many other cloud suppliers operating distributed, secure services at various cost levels and capabilities.

Foundation: An Information Security Policy

"Innovation is the outcome of a habit, not a random act." – Sukant Ratnakar

A Useful Template

Periodic Management Review and Signoff

Signature	Name	Position	Date

Purpose

The purpose of this document is to provide a broad framework of guidelines and defensive measures for the protection of company and customer information assets.

Its goal is to reduce the chances of a data breach, system hack, or privacy violation by mandating better practices, processes, monitoring and user education. Adopting these policies demonstrates to customers, employees and stakeholders that the company takes data security and privacy seriously. It provides a road map of how behaviors, procedures, protections and technology are used as added security measures.

It provides a high-level view of common threats and defensive measures, and the steps needed to better control risk. It strongly encourages the designation of specific staff or management to be responsible for certain tasks.

This policy document is considered effective when signed and dated by management, and may be revised, reviewed, and signed off on periodically in the future. This policy document should be updated at least quarterly, to ensure that the information is current. Verify that the correct individuals are still properly assigned to each area of responsibility, and that the identified responsibilities are being carried out.

Executive Summary

No security policy is 100% guaranteed to prevent a data breach or cyber incident. The threat landscape is constantly changing, and a dedicated team of hackers can eventually disrupt or gain access to operations and confidential data. What we will do is act to reduce the risks, and to do so cost-effectively.

Economics must be considered when implementing an Information Security Policy. The most elaborate defenses can be very costly. We will focus on those defensive measures which will provide the most impact at the least effort and cost. The "low hanging fruit" items will be addressed before more complex measures are considered.

Internal cyber threats have proven to be a greater risk than external threats. It is common to experience a data breach resulting from a bad actor guessing someone's password, or simply asking for it. Less common is the hooded hacker in a dark room delivering a complex technical exploit onto your network, although this does happen.

Therefore, policies and guidelines involving Account and Password Management and User Education are paramount, along with a current prioritized Data Inventory.

Policy statements and guidelines herein generally conform to the widely accepted NIST Cybersecurity Framework (National Institute of Standards and Technology).

Further steps which may bring additional security, albeit at an increased cost, are identified below under "Additional Steps".

Data Inventory

A thorough Data Inventory should be conducted and documented as part of the initial review of this policy document. All data – structured databases, text files, in-application data, spreadsheets, documents and images must be included.

Note where the data lives, how it's used, how it's protected, the owner, and the steward (who stores, backs up, and takes care of the data). Rank the data items in priority order. What are the "crown jewels"?

Review and update this inventory at lease annually, more often if data storage changes.

Use the form in Attachment A, and designate a responsible individual here.

Person responsible for implementing, verifying, and updating:	<<< *enter designated person here* >>>

Virtual Machines

With modern software tools, it is easy to create multiple virtual machines within one desktop computer, and even to have these machines run different operating systems. A Windows computer can easily host a Linux virtual computer on the same piece of hardware.

However, virtual machines on desktop computers create multiple security problems, including "VM proliferation". Such virtual computers may be forgotten (and their data forgotten as well) and thus not tracked. A virtual machine can be practically invisible to a user who is not intentionally accessing it.

Therefore, end users will not be authorized to create additional virtual machines on company computers without permission from IT. IT staff may create virtual machines on server hardware as needed, though care must be taken to include them in all inventory lists.

Desktop Applications, Flash Drives, CD Drives

No applications may be used on company desktop machines by end users, unless approved and installed by IT staff. If a laptop is brought into the office and connected to the network, either by WIFI or cable, its applications need to be reviewed by IT Staff before the device may access the network. Applications on laptops can harm the network or other machines on it.

Flash drives may be used to move data between machines only in emergencies, and when the responsible user is certain of exactly what is contained on the flash drive. CD drives should not be installed in, or used in, company machines.

Customize the Information Security Plan Here

<<< Consider adding more policy details concerning desktops and media devices >>>

| Person responsible for implementing, verifying, and updating: | <<< enter designated person here >>> |

Physical Security

The data center, or any location where routers, switches, and servers and housed, should be protected by a locked door requiring badge access to enter. If this is not possible, then a video recording device should be in place to record who has been in the location where this critical equipment resides.

Only IT staff and personnel with a need to access the servers and other network architecture should be in the vicinity. The data center or "server room" should not be a place for social activity or casual congregating.

Customer data should not be kept on portable laptops or tablets, which can be lost or easily stolen. Customer data should be kept on servers within the office network, or in a secure cloud location. If confidential, critical customer data is kept on a desktop computer then that computer must be carefully and verifiably added to the backup policy. The backups of these machines and all server backups should regularly be re-located to an off-site location or a cloud service for safekeeping or disaster recovery purposes.

Customize the Information Security Plan Here

<<< Consider adding additional details concerning desktops and media devices >>>

| Person responsible for implementing, verifying, and updating: | <<< *enter designated person here* >>> |

Backups / Ransomware

Ransomware involves a hacker taking control of a computer, encrypting all of the data, and demanding that a ransom be paid in order to unencrypt it. This is very damaging, and its greatest expense is usually the unavailability of data and software. Ransomware attacks are more likely to hit desktop and laptop computers than server machines.

The best defense against a devastating ransomware attack is a good backup regimen. The company should not pay the attackers' ransom. This is an easier guideline to follow if a recent data backup is available. Therefore, backups are critical.

Automatic Updates – the automatic loading and application of patches supplied by Microsoft - need to be activated on all desktop computers. Recent Windows versions (ex: Windows 10) have good protection against Ransomware when kept updated.

If possible, critical operating data should live on servers, not desktop machines, for easier backup and recovery.

Windows built-in backup service should be used to schedule automatic backups. IT staff may choose between full, incremental, and differential backup strategies. Differential backups are recommended, as the best compromise between resources required and the ability to recover from an incident. The backups should be taken at least weekly, and should be scheduled on a **daily basis** If data is changed every day.

Person responsible for implementing, verifying, and updating:	*<<< enter designated person here >>>*

Account and Password Policies

Microsoft Windows allows the system administrator to set password policies which the system will then enforce automatically. These should be the system password policies used:

- Minimum password length: Yes, 12 characters

- Maximum password age limit: No (NIST no longer recommends forcing a user to change her password periodically)

- Minimum password age limit: No (This is not needed)

- Password Complexity: Yes (User is required to use 3 of these 4 character types: small letters, capital letters, numbers, special characters)

Users are not encouraged to use excessive special characters or numbers in their password. Extremely complex passwords cause users to write passwords down and display them where others can see. A long password consisting of two unrelated words and a 2-4 digit number should work well. User passwords should not include their name, birthday, street, sports team, or other easily guessed words or numbers.

Default passwords on all devices should be changed, including routers and computers, Wireless Access Points, WIFI-enabled printers, and all other devices and Admin accounts. Default logins and passwords are a major threat to overall network and data security.

Automatic Updates

Every computer in the network should have its "Automatic Updates" feature enabled and should always include Security Updates being turned on as well. This allows the latest malware defenses and patches (small code fixes) to be installed into Windows automatically by Microsoft. Having current operating system software in place at all times protects each computer from ransomware and other attacks, and from new viruses and malware.

Person responsible for implementing, verifying, and updating:	<<< *enter designated person here* >>>

Malware Protection – Network vs. Standalone

Malware protection may be provided through a centralized network software tool that lets IT staff monitor and update the protections on each computer in the network. This strategy is an aid to efficiency and is recommended. The individual devices and computers are referred to as "endpoints" and these tools are called "endpoint protection" systems. There are many of these tools on the market. One example is the SEP (Symantec Endpoint Protection) system now sold and supported by Broadcomm. But there are other options, such as Bitdefender, Fortify, and Webroot.

Using a centralized tool is more efficient than having each user install his own malware protection. However, Microsoft Windows Defender may also be enabled on each computer to prevent malware infections. Recent Windows 10 versions now allow a device to have Windows Defender and a centrally-managed endpoint protection tool running at the same time. In the past, the SEP product would disable Windows Defender.

Current malware protection should be reviewed at least quarterly and protection for every computer should be verified.

Customize the Information Security Plan Here

<<< Consider adding additional details concerning anti-malware tools to be used >>>

Person responsible for implementing, verifying, and updating: | *<<< enter designated person here >>>*

User SAT

User Security Awareness Training (SAT) should be conducted at least annually. This can be done face-to-face or using a web based training solution. This training should be customized for the company's culture, operations, and industry, but a canned course can be purchased and delivered as an alternative.

Custom SAT courses can easily be developed in a streamlined learning platform such as FlexTraining (see FlexTraining.com), which provides authoring, delivery, tracking and testing. It can also deliver and track off-the-shelf courses.

This non-technical course is suitable for users and management at all levels. The purpose of the training is to reduce the chances of a successful attack or security breach, and to promote awareness of good security practices and habits.

An EXAMPLE SAT Course outline (edit or create your own):

1. Cyber Threats
2. Types of Attacks
3. Malware
4. Social engineering
5. Phishing, People
6. Physical Security
7. Password Management
8. Documents and Policies
9. Outside Devices and BYOD
10. Best Practices

Customize the Information Security Plan Here

<<< Describe your additional training needs: List subjects and audiences >>>

Person responsible for implementing, verifying, and updating: | <<< *enter designated person here* >>>

Acceptable Use Policy

An Acceptable Use Policy (AUP) will specify exactly what kinds of activity are allowed on the network and when using company equipment. **This policy will be developed jointly by IT staff and a representative from user management.** Violating the AUP will be grounds for dismissal. Each new employee will read and sign the AUP at the time of onboarding.

There should be a signed AUP on file for every employee and business partner who has access to the network.

Customize the Information Security Plan Here

<<< You may want to include your AUP or a suitable outline here >>>

Person responsible for implementing, verifying, and updating:	<<< *enter designated person here* >>>

Remote Access

Remote access technology allows employees to work from home or another location, and to connect to a desktop computer or other network component. This is an important enabling technology for a mobile or home-bound workforce. Two common methods which may be used to access the company network from home or another outside location are as follows:

1. Remote Desktop Protocol (RDP): The easiest and cheapest way to connect from home, it's built into Microsoft systems and is very popular. It is usually encrypted but is known to be somewhat vulnerable to hackers.

2. Virtual Private Network (VPN): This method offers encryption of data and login credentials moving in both directions, and is very secure. Employees working from a coffee shop or other public location should be using a VPN, since they will be utilizing an open wireless network – often with no encryption - in the public space.

Telnet and SSH should not be used for remote access for users. However, SSH has technical uses and may be deployed by IT personnel.

Person responsible for implementing, verifying, and updating:	*<<< enter designated person here >>>*

Incident Response (IR) Plan

An Incident Response Plan will be created, printed, reviewed and updated at least annually. The plan will formulate the initial response in the event of a data breach, a known privacy violation, theft of customer data, a denial-of-service attack, discovery of a remote access trojan, or other significant cyber incident. The plan will, at a bare minimum, include:

1. The names and contact information for every individual who needs to be notified.
2. What to shut down or disconnect to immediately limit the damage
3. Directions to verify the location and currency of backup data.
4. Data Inventory sheet created earlier.
5. Instructions for an initial meeting and identity of IR team members.
6. Additional elements and steps in the plan will be specific to the specific data and business operations involved, and the nature of the incident. For example, a ransomware attack response should include determining if the operating system was up-to-date and how a backup can be accessed to recover any lost data.

Customize the Information Security Plan Here

<<< Consider adding additional details for your Incident Response Plan >>>

Person responsible for implementing, verifying, and updating: *<<< enter designated person here >>>*

Web Site Location and Encryption

All company web sites and web-based applications (such as a policy update site or a quote generating application) should be hosted on a server outside the network. These applications and sites are "public-facing" and to have them on the internal network increases security risks. The web servers should be located inside a cloud service or in a co-location facility, where both the application servers and the database servers (which could be a single machine) can be completely separated from sensitive data on the company internal network.

It is possible that due to application and site design, sensitive data may reside on a public-facing server and be accessed by customers or prospects. For this reason, encryption should be utilized on any web or application server.

Encryption is accomplished using a signed digital certificate and a cryptographic protocol called TLS. TLS is often loosely referred to as "SSL", which is actually an older technology and the predecessor to TLS.

When TLS encryption has been properly set up on a server, the user's web browser establishes a trust relationship with the server, and the data moving in both directions is therefore encrypted.

Accessing a web site or application in encrypted mode uses "HTTPS" rather than "HTTP" in the web browser's location bar. The browser will also display an icon such as a closed padlock when the secure connection has been established,

The company servers will use TLS encryption at all times. Web sites should be designed and server options configured, to cause any HTTP request to automatically switch to the HTTPS method.

Customize the Information Security Plan Here

<<< Consider adding details about your organization's Web Sites & Applications >>>

Person responsible for implementing, verifying, and updating:	<<< enter designated person here >>>

Wireless Access Policies

Within the company office, any wireless service used to access the network must be using WPA2 encryption (not WPA or WEP). The WAP (Wireless Access Point) device should be configured to NOT broadcast the SSID. This step will make the WIFI service more difficult for a passing stranger to discover and connect to.

Away from the office, employees may need to use WIFI services at home or in a public setting (airport, café, etc.) to access the company network. In these cases, the user should be using the company VPN, which is managed by the VPN concentrator in the office. This maintains a secure, encrypted connection (a VPN "tunnel") between the user's computer or laptop and the office network at all times.

Customize the Information Security Plan Here

<<< Consider adding details about working from home and wireless devices >>>

| Person responsible for implementing, verifying, and updating: | <<< enter designated person here >>> |

Application and Web Deployment

All public-facing applications, including the company web site(s) should be located on servers outside of the company network. This must be the case whether the server is located in a cloud service or is company-owned, in which case it should be on a separate network from all desktop users, or placed at a co-location facility.

Network vs. PC Firewall (Windows Defender Firewall)

The network will be protected by a Firewall device, which will packet-filter all inbound traffic to the network. No traffic should be allowed to pass into the network without passing through the firewall device.

In order to provide maximum protection from malicious traffic, the firewall should be a modern "next gen" firewall, capable of "deep packet inspection".

To support the use of a VPN by at-home users, the firewall device should also be a "VPN concentrator". This means the device handles traffic and encryption for everyone connecting through a VPN tunnel. And this should include all remote traffic.

In addition, the Windows Defender Firewall on each desktop computer should be activated. This software-based firewall comes standard with Windows and is capable of rule-based port and protocol filtering.

Customize the Information Security Plan Here

<<< Consider adding details about your Firewall usage or non-windows defenses >>>

Person responsible for implementing, verifying, and updating: <<< enter designated person here >>>

Account Management

Every user will be given only the minimum permissions and access needed to do her job. Users who are not system administrators will not be given Administrative privileges.

System administrators will be issued two user accounts – one for normal activity, with normal permissions, and one "admin" account with system management authority for use when greater permissions are necessary.

No User Login should ever be shared with another user as this negates the ability to examine an audit trail of user activity and to maintain accountability.

User Logins will be disabled (not deleted) when an employee leaves the firm, so that log entries and history will be maintained.

Generic Guest passwords will not be used as they destroy the ability to determine exactly who did what on the system.

The network accounts should be audited at least quarterly to ensure compliance with these guidelines. On a Microsoft network, use of a domain controller can greatly aid in setting account policies and keeping track of user accounts and permissions.

Person responsible for implementing, verifying, and updating:	<<< *enter designated person here* >>>

Onboarding and Offboarding

Onboarding new hires will include having the employee read and sign an Acceptable Use Policy (AUP) for the network and company equipment. It will cover which activities are permitted on the network and which are not.

Offboarding will include disabling all user passwords utilized by the employee, and the removal of all company and customer data from the employee's laptop and mobile devices.

Customize the Information Security Plan Here

<<< Describe additional training or regulations for new hires or terminated staff >>>

Person responsible for implementing, verifying, and updating:	<<< *enter designated person here* >>>

Additional Steps, Resources Permitting

There are always additional measures and technologies which can be deployed in order to reduce cybersecurity risk. Some are fairly simple and inexpensive, while others are more elaborate and costly. With the average cost of a successful cyber attack estimated by CNBC at about $200,000, many of the available additional steps are at least worth considering:

Third party security assessment. An outside cybersecurity services company can be hired to examine policies, logs, procedures, and to run basic vulnerability scanning at a modest cost. The same company may be able to conduct user awareness (SAT) training.

Diagnostic scans and vulnerabilities. Periodically use the popular NMAP tool – an industry standard – to scan the network and servers. Use NMAP parameters to display connected devices, open ports, active applications, and even some known vulnerabilities. This can be done by internal IT staff or a third party.

More comprehensive vulnerability scanning. Very detailed vulnerability scanning may be performed if needed, using a specially designed vulnerability scanner such as Nessus or OpenVAS. Great care must be taken not to damage the network applications or impact current operations when using these tools.

SIEM (Security Information and Event Management). A software tool which aggregates server and network logs to form a unified view of network traffic and threats.

Useful if reviewing detailed logs is consuming a lot of staff time.

Packet Capture and Analysis. If malicious activity on the network is suspected, a powerful, flexible packet capture tool such as Wireshark can be used to examine traffic at a very detailed level. Must be performed using an in-house device.

Penetration Testing. This is an active attempt for an ethical "white hat" hacker to breach the network or access confidential data. Can be expensive, and is normally done by bigger companies who are very concerned about data security.

IDS/IPS (Incident Detection System / Incident Prevention System). Software tools that watch for anomalies or attacks. These might be part of the Next Gen firewall device discussed earlier, or they may run on a separate server. Considerable effort may be required to install and configure these systems.

NIST framework strict adoption. NIST offers a wealth of guidelines and standards, along with extensive documentation. A company with sufficient time and resources could benefit from a broad, comprehensive, adoption of NIST standards in all operational areas.

Disaster Recovery Plan. Every company should already have such a plan in place, but it needs to be consistent with the Incident Response plan above. It should include a Business Continuity Plan – which centers on the question "how do we keep operating with the loss of…" (the office, the electricity, our data, our computers, etc.)

Asset inventory. This is much like the Data Inventory above, only listing physical assets instead of data stores. What devices do we have, and how are we protecting them? Should include computers, laptops, tablets, mobile devices, routers, switches, printers, scanners, etc.

Consider Cyber Insurance. Insurance does not prevent cyber incidents, but it can certainly mitigate the financial loss associated with a breach or a successful attack. Carefully review terms and conditions to ensure coverages are appropriate and sufficient for your particular business or department.

Consider the ongoing Flex Protection *Defender* Program. For overall risk reduction, occasional scans and updates, and to maintain a basic relationship with a cybersecurity professional. The Defender program is a low-cost way to attain some additional peace-of-mind and keep up with trends and options.

*Note: This Information Security Policy should be considered a "living document". As such, it should be reviewed and modified on a regular basis. It is usable, and very useful, as is. The blue boxes above are merely opportunities for you to **customize your policy for your organization** and add details for individual policy areas. Technical skills are not required to add these kinds of details. If assistance is required in customizing this Information Security Plan or delivering end-user security awareness training, see www.flex-protection.com.*

The images at the top of the document may be replaced by your organization's logo at your discretion. This document may be shared with other companies, and departments.

Attachment A: Data Inventory Sheet [print copies and complete as needed].

[Consider adding "How Received" and "How Transmitted" columns]

Initials: _____

Data Store	Location / Who Uses	Steward	How Protected	Impact if Lost / Stolen
SAMPLE: Customer Master File	Main Office, Sales Server — Sales Reps	IT Dept, Server Team	Door keypad, Admin Login, Encryption	Sales activity disrupted, need to rebuild backup. Lose business to competitors. At least $100K lost.

Add A Security Charter Document

There is actually another document that is even more of a starting point than an ISP. Wait a minute. If the ISP is your foundation for everything else, then what can be under a foundation? In construction vernacular, let's think of it as a footer, or maybe a slab. In any event, it's called a Security Charter, and it answers really basic questions like "what are we doing?" and "why are we doing it?" and "who is involved"? It basically grants the authority for management to create and govern a data security program.

The contents of such a document vary widely from one company or organization to another. Therefore, it's not useful to try to offer a complete boilerplate example like we did for the ISP.

Instead, let's set our sights on a good Security Charter definition and outline that you can build on. Consider the initial question:

> For a medium sized company in the US, what items should be in the Information Security Charter document?

An information security charter is a high-level document that sets out the organization's approach to managing information security. The charter forms the foundation of the organization's information security program and communicates to all employees the importance the organization places on information security. It typically includes:

1. **Purpose:** An overview of why the organization has created an information security program and what it aims to achieve.

2. **Scope:** The scope should clearly define the areas of the organization where the information security policy applies. This usually covers all information systems, technologies, data, and users within the organization, whether they're permanent employees, contractors, or third-party suppliers.

3. **Objectives:** These are the goals the information security program seeks to achieve, such as protecting confidentiality, ensuring integrity, and maintaining the availability of the organization's information.

4. **Authority:** The charter should identify the executive sponsor(s) who has overall responsibility for information security in the organization, such as a Chief Information Security Officer (CISO) or similar role. The charter should also define the authority this role has, for example, to enforce policies and procedures.

5. **Responsibilities:** This section outlines the roles and responsibilities of different groups within the organization, such as the information

security team, IT department, human resources, and all employees.

6. **Policies and Standards:** An overview of the key policies and standards that support the information security program. This should include how these policies are enforced and the consequences of non-compliance.

7. **Risk Management Approach:** This defines the organization's approach to risk management, including how it identifies, assesses, responds to, and monitors information security risks.

8. **Incident Response:** The charter should explain the organization's approach to managing information security incidents, including roles and responsibilities during an incident and the steps taken to learn from incidents.

9. **Training and Awareness:** This section outlines how the organization will maintain an ongoing information security awareness and training (SAT) program.

10. **Review and Updates:** A commitment to regularly review and update the charter and the wider information security program to ensure it remains effective and aligned with the organization's objectives.

11. **Legal and Regulatory Compliance:** Mention the relevant legal, regulatory and contractual requirements the organization needs to meet, such as GDPR for companies dealing with EU citizens' data, HIPAA for healthcare data in the

US, or the requirements of PCI DSS for companies handling card payments.

Remember, an information security charter should be endorsed by senior management to show that the organization's leadership is committed to information security. It should also be communicated to all employees to ensure they understand the organization's approach to managing information security and their own responsibilities.

Never Overlook Training

"Technology is best when it brings people together."
– Matt Mullenweg

Security Awareness Training (SAT)

Training for users and for management is very important. Security professionals feel that there is no better return on investment than awareness training (often called SAT training). Recurrent training, in-person or online, has the best "bang for the buck". The exact course content will depend on your organization and its operating environment and culture. However, a good course outline might be similar to the following:

1. Phishing and social engineering: Teach employees how to recognize suspicious emails, phone calls, or messages that could trick them into revealing sensitive information.

2. Password security: Educate employees on creating and maintaining strong passwords, as well as the importance of using different passwords for different accounts.

3. Data protection: Emphasize the importance of safeguarding sensitive data, including personal identifying information (PII), financial data, and customer information.

4. Mobile device security: Discuss best practices for securing mobile devices, including setting passcodes, encrypting data, avoiding public Wi-Fi, and downloading apps from trusted sources.

5. Social media usage: Highlight the risks associated with posting sensitive personal or corporate information on social media, and teach employees how to protect their online identities.

6. Physical security: Educate employees on the importance of securing physical devices and data, including locking doors, shredding sensitive documents, and using secure file cabinets.

7. Incident response: Explain what employees should do in the event of a security breach or incident, including who to contact and what steps to take to minimize damage and prevent future incidents.

8. Web browsing: Teach employees how to stay safe when browsing the internet, including avoiding suspicious or unsecured websites, downloading antivirus software, and using browser plugins like ad blockers and password managers.

9. Remote work: With the rise of remote work, it's important to educate employees on best practices for working securely from home or other remote locations. This could include using virtual private networks (VPNs) to protect data, securing home Wi-Fi networks, and keeping work devices separate from personal devices.

10. Email safety: In addition to phishing and social engineering, there are several other email-related security risks to be aware of, such as email spoofing, attachment-

based malware, and email bombing. Train employees to recognize these threats and take steps to mitigate them.

11. Cybersecurity regulations: Depending on the industry your organization operates in, there may be specific regulations or compliance requirements to be aware of. Make sure employees understand these requirements and how to comply with them.

Overall, the goal of a Security Awareness Training course should be to help employees understand how cybersecurity threats work, what they can do to protect themselves and their organization, and how to respond in the event of a security incident. By providing regular training and education on these topics, you can help create a stronger security culture and reduce the risk of data breaches and other cyber incidents.

Training for Executives

Executives and upper-level managers, and board members for that matter, are not the target of SAT training. That's for all internal system users, and for third party supply chain users as well.

Who makes policy? Who sets the tone, and the security culture at a company or government department? Who provides ongoing leadership? Are these folks automatically equipped to handle these important security roles, or is training needed?

Of course it is needed, and the subject matter needs to be greatly different from the SAT course outlined above. It also needs to be different from the detailed, technical material and lessons that make up the training taken by security professionals and technicians. An executive does not need to know how to install and operate the Wireshark packet sniffer software, for example.

The CISM (Certified Information Security Manager) industry certification follows a subject matter outline that is largely suitable for this target audience. It tends to focus more on governance, documentation, and verbiage, rather than technical concepts and details. I know from experience that the material in this certification can be a bit dry.

I have seen commercial executive training, closely following the CISM outline, labelled as 'Cyber Security for the Boardroom" and delivered in a one-day compressed format. Seems to be a bit too brief, to me. The point is that some kind of management-oriented security training needs to be part of the training picture, for almost any sized organization.

We'll talk more about the suggested curriculum for this training in a few chapters. But here is a sample description from a provider who offers "Executive and Managerial" training for state and local government employees:

> *Half-day, one-day, and two-day courses that cover topics like cyber risk management and incident response and business continuity planning.*

If You Can Only Do X Things

"We're still in the first minutes of the first day of the Internet revolution." – Scott Cook

It's not a great approach to information security, but for many small and medium organizations, there is no place else to start. I am going to suggest – in summary form - what actions you can take if you have an extremely limited time and budget.

So, with apologies to anyone who likes to be thorough and comprehensive, here we go:

If you only have the time to do one thing. (No, we aren't going there. You need at least two.)

If you only have time to do 2 things:

1. Set password policies across the network for length and complexity. This is a technical control, but it pays dividends. No more "William" or "123456".

2. Conduct some form of SAT training for users –
    cyber hygiene, password management, just the
    basics.

If you have time for only 3 things:

Create a formal Information Security Policy and have
management sign off on it. Now you have an approved
roadmap to guide the rest of your security rules and
activities. A larger company will even create a "Security
Charter" document which establishes the need for data
security management and establishes basic roles and
responsibilities. Include automated backups – what, when,
and who is responsible!

If you only have time for 4 things:

Add in an Information Asset Inventory. What are you
protecting? Where are all your information stores, how
they are protected, and what happens if they are destroyed
or leaked? Start with the most important items (maybe a
customer list or financial data) and prioritize from there. I
have read of a large enterprise who consumed over a year
of work for a whole team on just this task. For most
companies, it will be a bit easier. Include employees'
laptops!

If you have time for only 5 things:

Create a realistic Incident Response Plan. This can be
elaborate or very simple, or somewhere in between. Even
the bare-bones "who to call, what to tell them, and what to
do next" is much better than nothing.

If you have time for only 6 things:

Conduct formal executive security training, giving the management team the tools and tactics they need to manage the overall security effort. Yes, ideally this would be done before anything else, but that's probably not realistic. The five items above are critical and really should take precedence.

If you only have time for 7 things:

Acquire and activate firewalls. Acquire a firewall device that guards the perimeter of the network and filters traffic coming in and out. The "Next Generation Firewall" has lots of intelligence and can store malware definitions to help block them. (Renew your malware definitions regularly). And the personal firewall (software) on every desktop machine should be activated as well. It can take some time to learn and set all the rules in both of these firewalls.

If you only have time to do 8 things:

Consider hiring or appointing a dedicated CISO (Chief Information security Officer) to head the security initiative. For a small company, an IT manager may have this role as part of her job.

If you only have time for 9 things:

Take a look at your physical security. Certainly you have doors and locks, but who has the keys? Who can get to the data center and your servers? Are badges being used effectively? Has anyone gotten past a secure door without one? Does your staff let strangers walk in?

If you only have time for 10 things:

Consider deploying additional technical tools or software:

A. A SIEM is an excellent software tool that combines and summarizes network and server traffic and alerts you of exceptions or anomalies that you need to know about.

B. An IPS (Intrusion Prevention System) can monitor the network and keep harmful malware out. Be aware that this functionality may also be included in your firewall device itself.

C. An asset management console (my name for tools like Bit Defender) is a dashboard-based system to help you view your whole network and determine the status, patch history, and any problems for all assets you are managing. Seeing everything in one place is a good start, and you can drill down for more details if there are issues or red flags.

OK, that's enough of that. It's a very blunt approach to developing a security plan. But those are defenses and controls that can help you stay safe, listed in priority order, according to my experience and opinion.

What am I leaving out? A ton of controls, tools, and defensive measures. For many companies, mainly larger enterprises, there is a need to:

1. Engage in formal Penetration Testing ("pen-testing") which would involve "ethical hacking". It may include a red team (attackers), a blue team (defenders), and a purple team (reviewing the exercise afterward for lessons learned). Or for a smaller company, a single outside resource might be hired, or internal IT staff.

    Entire books have been written about pen testing. If you have a security role in a large enterprise you can expect to engage in a pen testing project at some point, and you should do some reading to prepare.

2. Create and manage your own "certificates" to aid in encryption and decryption. This can get complicated, but to simplify, every machine can have one or more certificates that allow it to serve and receive encrypted data, ideally in an end-to-end encryption scheme.

    Public and private encryption keys are used, and individuals can have certificates as well. You are probably using certificates every time you access the web today, but you just don't see them. There are settings in your web browser that help dictate just how encryption and certificates are handled.

3. Possibly hire outside companies to do consulting projects, vulnerability assessment, and just about anything security-related. For example, there are services and software that track how your users are

doing on resisting the habit of clicking on email attachments and malicious links. Fake malware and fake phishing emails are used and there are even scores given to each user. A high-end option would be to hire an MSSP to constantly monitor every device (or "endpoint") in your organization.

4. Utilize a "packet-sniffer" application to analyze network traffic at a very detailed level. The most popular packet sniffer is called Wireshark, and it's a powerful, flexible set of filters and screens that can easily inundate you with information. Know that using Wireshark requires you to actually be sitting in the network or subnet you are focusing on. It's not really a remote tool.

   If you suspect that malware or malicious traffic is a problem on your company's network, Wireshark is a way to confirm it. You can examine individual TCP/IP data packets, as well as groups of transmissions and packets, known as "conversations". Expect a ramp-up period as you master the screens, filters and display options in this robust application.

5. Utilize a VPN (Virtual Private Network) when you connect to your workplace desktop or server from home or a coffee shop. You really need to use a VPN, for many reasons. Among other things, it provides an end-to-end "tunnel" that keeps your login, password, and data encrypted.

   It's common to use RDP (Remote Desktop Protocol) to connect to work from your laptop. But using it from an airport or other public place with public WiFi is risky. So, you can combine a VPN and RDP to keep your logins and data secure. Start up the VPN, then start the RDP client and make the connection. In the office, on a desktop machine or within a firewall device, will be an RDP "host" which lets authorized users in.

6. And there are more tools and services available every year. Security technology is definitely a growing market.

As the saying goes, your results may vary. Be aware that there are a plethora of useful and sophisticated tools and services that are available depending on your organization's budget.

But even if you don't end up adopting these advanced practices and technologies, it pays to be aware of them and to gather information from the web and YouTube on how they work.

Here is where we remind ourselves that the simpler steps listed at the beginning of this chapter are our focus and are very much worth doing. Let's call them the "low hanging fruit" and re-dedicate ourselves to getting these simpler, cheaper things done first.

Role of AI and ChatGPT

"The real danger is not that computers will begin to think like men, but that men will begin to think like computers." – Sydney J. Harris

A Limited Overview

It seems like you can't turn on a TV or a phone these days without hearing some news about Artificial Intelligence. AI is the current buzzword for almost all situations, with many business software tools and services described as "Powered by AI". Microsoft has invested several billion dollars in AI development and marketing. So that tells you the big players are serious about it.

OK, they invested a lot of money in Internet Explorer too, and that did not end well. But nobody gets it right every single time.

Before we talk about how you might use AI in your data security work, let's talk about what AI is, from a simplified viewpoint. And let's use ChatGPT as our example, since it seems to be the most commonly used technology in this area.

ChatGPT is a "natural language processor". At its core, it turns language into different language, or into images. Hmmmmm. OK, let's talk about the "how". AI uses "deep learning", reading through billions of media items, web pages and documents, to train itself.

But in my view, it doesn't really "know" anything. It doesn't even really understand words. It understands fragments of words, and it knows how to assemble them, based on what it has seen others do, and can thus form conversations. If they are poorly trained, ChatGPT and other AI tools will give poor results/answers. AI is not much on judgement and fairness.

You communicate with ChatGPT using "prompts", which may be questions or sets of instructions. You type a prompt in a window, and wait a few seconds, and back comes a reply, which usually makes sense and honors your instructions. For many AI tools, it could be an image or a video, since those formats can be created as well.

We can't really claim to be presenting a well-rounded overview of AI here. That would take much more time and effort, for certain. We are barely scratching the surface. So, before we get off the rails, let's slow down and consider a really simple example usage of ChatGPT.

Assume you have a window open in your web browser where you can send a prompt to ChatGPT (Yes, OpenAI.com has a "playground" web page for this purpose – check it out)

You could have a bit of fun. Send a prompt like "Write a song about Bob Smith, a lawyer who likes iced tea and football" or use yourself or a friend's name. And you would get back, in a few seconds, a song with multiple versus and probably a chorus. You may need to supply your own music, but it's usually a pretty good effort.

This exercise may relax you in the face of the coming global doom that some people see as the invasion of AI. Is this good practice for a beginner learning how AI works? I think so, but there are many other options.

So, let's send in the identical prompt again. What comes back is not the same song as what it gave you a moment ago. What? I thought computers were good at following instructions, and generating the same text again and again under the same conditions. What's going on?

Well, there is a parameter (you can sometimes control it, sometimes not, depending on your web interface) called "temperature". If the temperature parameter is set to 0, you will get an identical, or nearly identical, reply to a certain prompt every time. But if the temperature is closer to 1.0, like perhaps 8.5, the results will vary widely, as ChatGPT uses its imagination and changes things up.

Well, let's pull the plug on our AI overview at this point. I encourage you to explore AI in books, YouTube videos, websites like OpenAI.com, and in other ways. No matter how you earn a living, you will be dealing with AI in one form or another for a long time.

I am all for having the government regulating how AI and ChatGPT are used, but it's definitely not going away. So have some fun with it and become a knowledgeable user. It will give you confidence and may even help lighten your workload in some way. It's good at information-based work and language processing, and you have probably heard about college students using AI to write their essays. It does a great job of performing those kind of tasks.

Simple Info Security Uses

The most basic and obvious usage for AI in Information Security is the creation of content. Consider two examples using ChatGPT and remember that an AI prompt is not a Google search. You are looking to create content, not a list of web pages that may be useful.

One use would be to help develop your foundation security documents. So a possible prompt might be "Create a Information Security Policy". Does ChatGPT know what an Information Security Policy is? Can it create one? Yes, and yes.

But let's improve our prompt. How about "Create an Information Security Policy for a local government with 500 users on Windows computers"? Or a multi-national enterprise, or a franchise with high turnover?

And you can create an outline for your custom Security Awareness Training course in the same manner. Maybe your first prompt is something like "Create an outline for a security awareness training for end users." You will get a reply which may be useful as a starting point to create such a course.

But let's improve our prompt again. How about "Create an outline for a security awareness training course for 100 end users in a large grocery store."? Or a manufacturer, or a consulting firm?

And when it's time to develop the details each lesson in such a course (maybe a lesson on password management) who will you turn to? Yes, ChatGPT can be useful at a detailed level as well.

These are just two examples from many possibilities. The point is, the more information you give in your prompt, the better and more useful the response will be.

This is where I have to remind you that AI, whether it's ChatGPT or another tool, is not perfect. It makes mistakes, it can be biased, and it's sometimes just wrong. So, it's up to you, the human, to review and modify everything you get from AI, as needed.

For instance, a few weeks ago, I was using an AI image generation tool to create photo-like images for a client's website. You get the idea – I prompt it with something like "create a high-resolution picture of some executives sitting around a boardroom table" and it gives me an image, or actually several images. Cool!

But wait, what's this? Are there people in these images with one eye missing, and others who seem to have lost their chins? A man who is wearing half a pair of glasses? During one session, the best photo image I got was man reading through a folder. He looked good, but he did have six fingers. These are not handicapped people; these are errors. So be careful and remember that you, not AI, are responsible for your work product.

Complex Info Security Uses

M any examples are available, but one favorite involves examining the flow of internet and intra-net traffic and looking for anomalies. On a PC level, consider the traditional anti-malware tools and imagine their ability to see every packet of data going in both directions. If it has been trained to know what malware looks like in general, and how it behaves, that would be very useful. As it is now, anti-malware software has to have a massive list of all the malware out there, so it can see if any of the culprits are on the local machine.

And Intrusion Detection Systems (IPS) and Intrusion Prevention Systems (IPS) work the same way – AI helps them detect suspicious transactions. This is a leap forward from the older "list-based" processes. For added convenience, the functionality of IDS and IPS systems can often be found on advanced or "Next Generation" firewalls rather than implemented as a separate product. But the same idea applies.

Other security tools, like SIEM systems, Asset Tracking Systems, and Vulnerability Scanner Software are already making use of AI in their own way, as well.

Exactly how AI is applied to improve scanning and recognition of incidents, issues, malware and other details is beyond the scope of this discussion. But know that it's happening, and that part of the job of the security professional is knowing how the pieces fit together. Understanding AI is one thing. Being able to deploy and configure it (and to train an AI tool before it's useful, for that matter) is another thing entirely.

In a commercial sense, let's all agree that AI is not just a technical solution and security filter. It's also a marketing factor. At recent conferences and trade shows, I have seen many claims of "AI-based" and AI powered" solutions. However, the target audience, the potential buyers, often have no idea what that means. But it sounds good, and do you want to be the security software provider who is behind the times?

Prompt Engineering

Your prompts, the text you submit to your chosen AI tool so it can properly create the text or image response that you need, are incredibly important. They need to be given a lot of thought beforehand, and some trial and error can be expected.

In the context of this discussion, it is almost unfortunate that we have all been Googling for 15 years or so. We are accustomed to tossing out a couple of words, or maybe a half-dozen, and letting Google build us a list of resources from there. We all have expectations based on this experience.

Using Siri or Google Assistant doesn't change things much. You still usually keep it short and sweet, and hope you get back a useful answer. A request like "Siri, which teams are in the AFC North in NFL football?" is actually a longer than average question in this regard.

Of course, an AI tool like ChatGPT needs a bit more. Put yourself in its place (If we are going to treat AI like humans then maybe you can consider yourself an AI robot, just for a moment). You have a vast storehouse of data and have been exhaustively trained.

But what are you going to do with this prompt:

"Create an orientation course outline for new hires."

You have really not been given enough information. Some guessing and a lot of assumptions would have to go into creating a response for your user. Fortunately, ChatGPT handles "conversations", so it remembers what you have submitted from one prompt to another. So, a user can narrow her request down with additional prompts, which is helpful.

On the other hand, maybe the user could start with a more thorough prompt in the first place. How about this one:

"Build a detailed outline for an orientation course for new employees and contractors for a large manufacturer of cosmetics in the United States."

We could continue in this manner. But the point is that the more information and instructions in your request (your "prompt") the more the AI engine can compare it with its vast internal references. And thus, a more complete prompt results in a better, more detailed, more thorough response.

Using words like "reply" and "response" for the result of your request does not really do justice to the complexity of what's being done. This is especially true if we are requesting images, audio, or video. Maybe the term "work product" should be used now and then.

Creating good and productive prompts is now a recognized skill set, and as such has been dubbed "prompt engineering". This is a useful term in my view, because it reflects the effort and even the structural development that goes into creating good AI prompts. Something good to have on your resume, as long as you can back it up.

There are also books on the subject of prompt engineering, and they are loaded with good examples. The ones I have read through were easy reads and were very clear on what they were telling you. If your job or consulting engagement involves using ChatGPT or a similar tool on a regular basis, I recommend you acquire one of these books and keep it handy.

When you start to read more deeply about prompt engineering, you may be shocked. I know I was. ChatGPT is extremely conversational and detailed, and dare I even say "lifelike"? You might decide to start your prompt with something like "Pretend you are my lawyer", and then request that some kind of contract or agreement be created. Your response will generally contain something like the caveat "I can't create anything that is legally binding" before it suggests some questions or factors you may want to consider.

Talking like a lawyer while stating that it cannot be a lawyer – that's just about what I would call "self-awareness". Ask it how to install a new muffler on your old Mustang convertible, and a whole different personality will emerge. This thing is not perfect, you remind yourself. But given a good prompt it's pretty darn useful. And versatile to boot!

By the way, I am using ChatGPT as an example far too much. There are many other AI solutions out there in the marketplace, and there will be even more in the future. You can find several AI tools that are apps for your cell phone, for both IOS and Android. Some are free and some are "free-ish" (ads, premium upgrades, limitations etc.).

Development of the landscape of AI tools is just getting started. I reference ChatGPT a lot because it's popular, accessible, and easy to use. But consider experimenting with other tools before you get locked into just one. The AI world is not just ChatGPT.

One Last AI Example

Let's have some fun. Can you identify the small section in the preceding pages (It's about one page long) that was written, not be me, but by ChatGPT? Please don't read ahead on this page as you look for this section. OK – did you find it yet?

Look back at the section titled "A Security Charter Document". After the introductory paragraph, locate the question that begins with "For a medium sized company...".

You got it – that question was used as a prompt to ChatGPT. And the outline that follows is what ChatGPT returned. Does it stick out as being written in a different style than the sections and pages around it? Maybe the answer to that question is subjective.

It's expected that you will typically need to edit whatever ChatGPT creates for you. But in this case, I left it alone. And the summary at the bottom of the outline was courtesy of ChatGPT as well.

It's nothing amazing or groundbreaking, I admit. But it's a nice example of how useful these tools are, and how they can be great timesavers. To be honest, I though the outline above should have mentioned the important ISP document, since it's authorized and supported by the Charter. But that's just my opinion, so I left it alone.

Risk Assessment and Management

A Lightning-Fast Risk Assessment

If you are in the early days of building an Info security program, you may want to start out with the question "How much risk is present that just comes with our normal day-to-day operations"? Or perhaps "Are we set up to keep risk to a minimum, or do our normal practices make things harder?"

This mini-assessment tool is a good fit for small or medium business or nonprofits or government departments. If you already have a robust, mature security program at your workplace you may not get much out of this exercise.

In that spirit, let's do what I hope is the world's fastest cybersecurity risk assessment. Here is how it works:

Each question has three possible answers. For each question, the first candidate answer indicates the least risk and the last answer indicates the highest risk. And of course, the answer in the middle points at moderate risk. Give yourself a "2" for every time you select the first answer. Award a score of "1" for the second answer and "0" for the third answer. There are nine questions here.

The best possible score is therefore 18 and the score indicating the highest overall risk will be 0. That score would require you to select the most risky answer for each and every question.

If you can honestly choose the first answer for every question, your assessment score will be 18. That's good. A lower total score indicates a less secure posture, and therefore higher risk. It doesn't mean your company is incapable of managing a good security program. It just means your security practices, and your operations, are pointing to a higher overall risk of data breaches or cybersecurity incidents.

This assessment works great online, with dropdown answer lists and automated scoring, but it works fine here too. With that understanding, take a look at the questions below and note your accurate response to each. Then add up your score.

Question	Select an Answer
Do you have a written Information Security Policy that is endorsed by management?	Yes No Not sure
How often are employees and management given Security Awareness Training (SAT)?	At least annually Now and then Never
Do you have a documented Data Inventory - a list of key data stores, where they are located, and how they are protected?	Yes and it's current Yes but it's outdated No such inventory
Is there a convenient list of Security Best Practices that all users are familiar with?	Yes, everyone is familiar A few people use such a list No such list here
Is critical data backed up automatically, onto separate computers used for backups?	Yes, automated and verified Manual backups, frequently Backups are infrequent at best
Does your company have remote or traveling employees who need network access?	No, everyone works on site Yes, and we use a secure VPN Many remote workers, no VPN

Have you had a network vulnerability scan or professional security assessment from an outside consultant or advisor?	Yes, on a regular basis Yes, but not lately Never
Does your company or organization have a public-facing web site?	No website Public website on an external server Public website on our internal network
Do you have a centralized console or Data Defender subscription to ensure Security Best Practices?	Yes, robust security platform/console in place Basic asset tracking and consolidated logging No such software or console

The lower your score, the more "opportunities" you have to improve your security posture. Of course, some factors – like remote employees – are just a fact of life and can't really be changed.

Risk Management: With the Numbers

Risk management, done in a formal manner, starts with assessing the annual cost of each potential risk. How do you do that? Here are some standard acronyms and definitions (simplified that will lead you to the annual cost of a given risk. And the cost leads you to a decision about how much money you may be willing to spend to mitigate or eliminate this risk.

So here goes:

ARO: Annual rate of occurrence. How often do you expect the event to occur? For example, how often does your main web server get taken over by a ransomware attack? Or how often does one of your field sites catch on fire? Perhaps a given event happens three times per year.

SLE: Single Loss Expectancy. How much damage is done, in terms of money, every time the event occurs? It may be that, on average, each time the risk manifests itself and the negative event occurs, it costs you $200,000.

ALE: Multiply the ARO by the SLE and you get your ALE, the Annual Loss Expectancy. If this event happens three times a yarer and it costs you $200,000 in repair costs and lost business each time, then your ALE is $600,000. So, the amount you would be willing to spend to eliminate this risk might be $600,000 annually.

But hold your horses. Do you really know the full cost of recovering from this event? And how confident are you in your "three times a year" forecast? If you make major decisions based on your calculated ALE, and one of your inputs (ARO and SLE) are way off, you need to be careful. "Garbage in, garbage out" is a good warning to heed here.

I am not saying that calculating your annual expected loss for a given risk using the conventional techniques above is a waste of time. On the contrary, I think it's an important exercise and can be a real eye-opener when trying to identify your most dangerous risks. But understand the accuracy of your numbers and if necessary, take your results with a grain of salt.

Risk Management: Without the Numbers

Let's assume that you are not yet in a position to estimate the cost of repair and the opportunity cost of lost business for most of your data security and other operating risks. You can't confidently provide numbers for your ARO and SLE, because both values are unpredictable, or you are in a new line of business, or whatever. Taking wild guesses and doing the math may not be your only option.

Instead, let's turn to a tried and true, and extremely simple, technique that has been used to support all kinds for management decisions for decades, if not longer. We'll call it an "opportunity graph", and it works like this:

Draw a basic 2-dimensional graph, with a vertical axis at the left and a horizontal axis across the bottom. Label the vertical axis as "Likelihood" and the horizontal axis as 'Damage". Think of the open area between the axes as being divided into 4 quadrants. You might look at them as being Northwest, Northeast, Southwest and Southeast.

At the bottom of the Likelihood axes you can place the label "Unlikely" and at the top "Very Likely". And the "Damage" axis labels could run from left to right as "Little Damage" to "Devastating".

In any event, plot your perceived security risks in the graph in one of the four quadrants, based on what you know about them. In the Northeast quadrant you will find the risks that most need managing and mitigation. These must be given priority and here would be where you would invest your money and apply the strongest security controls. These are your most important "opportunities".

As an illustration, imagine that you have had problems over the years with password management and social engineering. Users have chosen weak passwords, given them out to co-workers frequently, and also to outsiders with bad intentions. As a result, several data breaches have occurred, at great cost to your company. The frequency of these attacks varies greatly from year to year, and the cost can be much higher in some cases than in others.

Thus, this "opportunity graph" technique will have in its Northeast corner something like "Poor Password Management" or "Social Engineering". It's highly likely, and it's costly. Based on that, these issues are assigned a high priority. You may choose to implement a technical control such as stricter password rules (length, content, etc.). Or an administrative control such as regular training for all users on how to defend against social engineering attacks.

This technique is not rocket-science. It's a simple way to identify which risks deserve the most attention and why. There is no reason you can't deploy both of the above tactics to identify your most critical risks. Just be careful with the numbers on the first process.

Parting Shots – Thoughts on Key Issues

"Just because something doesn't do what you planned it to do doesn't mean it's useless." – *Thomas Edison*

What follows is a sampling of various articles I have written over the last few years. There may be some overlap with the preceding material, but mainly in cases where I feel like a certain concept or action is really important.

I don't like kicking a dead equine, but if I will leave you with two thoughts, they are:

1. There are a LOT of steps you can take to improve your data security without busting your budget or disrupting your business.

2. You need to do something to get your arms around this issue – security and breaches – as soon as you can. Something!

In that way, these excerpts should fit with the spirit and overall themes of the rest of the book.

Information Security After the Pandemic

In the age of Covid-19, it was certainly not business as usual. But there are still hackers and bad actors out there doing their work, in the US and globally. So what impact, if any, did the pandemic have on the world of cyber security and best practices? Here are a few ways, and this is by no means an exhaustive list.

First and foremost, company focus will have shifted to personal safety, worker well-being, and in many cases out-and-out survival. Can we assume that every single data security best practice will be followed all the time, when so many other things are at risk? For example, should we expect every employee or business partner to successfully resist social engineering attacks when she is also engaged in social distancing and wiping down everything she touches? Social engineering – fooling a human into giving you what you want - is still going on, and will always be a major threat.

Thus, the biggest change and increase in data security risk is thus an understandable shift in daily focus, at all levels from the boardroom to the breakroom, or into people's homes as stay-at-home policies dictate. Good data security requires a strong security culture, and that culture may have taken a hit in recent years, in many cases.

Secondly, good information security costs money. The US federal government has been throwing around a lot of cash to stem the bleeding. But many companies, especially small and mid-market concerns, are likely to be working with tight budgets for a while, considering the recent recession. And the situation may be even worse for state and local governments, who are bearing so much of the pandemic burden.

We're talking about money for staff, technology, software updates, better firewalls and detection software, consulting services, and of course user training. The financially strapped company or local government may have to make some difficult choices.

For example, we know of situations where budget issues have forced a CIO to serve as CISO when a dedicated CISO would have been preferred. This choice may not only reduce the resources directed toward data security. They may also take the CIO away from his customary role in policy development and planning.

Third, let's consider endpoint security. An endpoint is basically a desktop PC used by an employee, or a tablet or even a mobile device. And let's remember that many people are still working from home now, a practice that may last a while.

It is fairly likely that a team member's desktop at the office would be pretty well "hardened" with the latest software updates, a software firewall, and anti-virus protection. And perhaps the CD/DVD and USB interfaces have been disabled in the name of malware prevention.

But what's available at home?

The home computer utilized during this emergency may be a whole different ballgame. It may have an older operating system, discontinued software updates, games, custom screen-savers that the kids like, and a whole host of other vulnerabilities. Is customer data being loaded into this vulnerable machine? Is it left on overnight?

Fortunately, if user training has been done properly, online best practices should come home with the displaced user. These practices would be basically unchanged as the employee logs in from home. But there is a lot less control over the device itself when it's remote, or at least a different way of implementing it.

Many employees will try and utilize their mobile devices as their "home computer", but in spite of the habits of the younger generation, I don't view a phone as a computer. A mobile phone on WiFi (or even 4G/5G) has its own set of security concerns, a tiny screen and keyboard, and limited functionality as well.

There will be other changes as the population at the office stays small and quiet for a period. For instance, all the physical security measures – guards, motion-sensors, man-traps, swipe cards - will be less important, less utilized, and in the long term may be reduced. But they will still be needed.

Finally, it is well known that the greatest danger to a company's information security is the "disgruntled employee". The damage an insider can do is almost unlimited. In times of great stress, both personal and economic, will there me more or fewer such employees? Only time will tell.

Making Cyber Security Easier

Everyone talks about cybersecurity and how important it is, even in tough times. But until your company or local government gets hit by hackers or suffers a data breach, most companies don't do much about it.

As far as preparation and prevention, what can you do? Where do you start? How do you avoid having your budget drained by a smooth-talking consulting firm? The key is to understand that there are simple, economical defenses and improvements that will make a real difference.

Let's take a quick look at some factors to consider.

First, who needs to give data security a priority? Maybe not everyone. We tell our friends and contacts in various business to ask themselves if they fit any or most of the following drivers, before they ask us for help. Is this you?

- We want to improve data security while staying within a budget.
- We could use help developing or reviewing a formal data security policy.
- We need a method to inventory our critical data and where it's located.
- We could use a detailed plan for threat assessments and active security testing.
- We are looking for vulnerability scanning and penetration testing to identify possible exposures.
- We need to get our arms around the most critical risks and how to reduce them.
- We may soon be moving our data and systems into the cloud.
- We want to reduce risks by providing Best Practices education for our end users.

- We want to know what modern tools and systems are available for protecting our data.
- We could use a brief "discovery" conversation to identify options.

What's the desired outcome? In many cases, mid-level management wants to be able to show "C" suite management that they are doing SOMETHING. Being caught totally unprepared, and having made no effort, when a data breach happens is beyond embarrassing.

That's not a very ambitious goal, but it's a starting point. There are copious resources available online, include a wall-to-wall comprehensive collection of documentation and controls from NIST, a framework provided by the federal government. Broad, deep, and rich in content, it's a great resource for heavy-hitters and large security teams.

But let's boil it way down, and identify two actions you can take today, before you jump up to run to your next meeting:

So, read through the framework at NIST (www.nist.gov). Expect to spend 90 minutes reading it and 1-5 days following up, if you follow its guidelines. There is no simpler, common-sense way to move towards the goal of better protecting your information assets.

Don't have 90 minutes? Here is the second suggested action: Keep reading.

Below are seven "best practices" that will help keep you out of trouble in the long run (no system or company is 100% protected, of course):

1. Have a comprehensive, documented Information Security Policy.

Yes, even a small company, a non-profit association, or a small government department should have such a policy. Here is where you will identify strategies, practices, and rules to help avoid data breaches and compromised systems. You won't know where you stand or where you are going without a road map.

2. Spend the most resources on protecting the crown jewels. (Create an asset inventory so you know what you have to protect.)

Determine which systems, databases, and networks have the most critical data, the stuff you cannot operate without. And direct your efforts and resources toward protecting these assets.

One good tactic is to draw out a graph with the "importance of data" along one axis and with "effort/cost to protect" on the other. Then plot your systems and potential projects on the graph, and focus your protection resources on the Low Cost / High Importance data items. For example, strengthening password policies does not cost much and can have a big impact.

This technique is probably the oldest and simplest analytic tool to identify priorities, but that's because it works.

3. Place a high priority on user education.

Most data breaches and security problems can be traced to failure to observe sensible practices, or to understand the impact of certain habits. In fact, there are many user habits and practices that can create an exposure that leads to serious breaches.

Yes, there are also purely technical attacks that can infiltrate your network and do great harm. But user education – and online testing with E-learning – can greatly enhance the security awareness level of management and end-users. And user education generally produces a lot of "bang for the buck" compared to any other activity. Social engineering is still the biggest threat or "attack vector" as it is sometimes called.

4. Consider Hiring a Penetration Tester.

Or designate an internal resource – probably an IT professional - to take on that role. A "pen tester" will know how to use software tools to test for vulnerabilities and even launch attacks against your servers or network (while doing no actual damage). Make sure there is a mutual, documented understanding from the outset about what is to be tested and how to protect (and back up) live data to minimize risk.

5. Separate computers, networks, and servers when possible.

If you operate a web server, try to keep it on a different network from the one your users are on. Your web site WILL BE attacked regularly, and you don't want a successful hacker fishing around in your user's computers. For similar reasons, keep applications and databases on different machines. Keeping your public-facing systems in the cloud may also help in some cases, but that may not be ideal for other reasons.

6. Get cost-effective help.

Completing any form at Flex-protection.com (or some other InfoSec consultant's website) will get you to a quick and useful "discovery conversation", and that's a good first step. And there are loads of cyber security experts out there, at various costs. Build a long-term relationship based on common-sense practices and improvements. When a consultant makes recommendations, they should make sense to you, and no project should disrupt your business and make your life more complex.

Share the burden of figuring everything out and building a better set of policies and defenses. You will soon find that there are many good industry best practices beyond the examples listed here.

7. Stay with it.

No one wants to be the CEO, VP, or Director who passed up a chance to increase data security and then got hacked. So most leaders are at least willing to seriously consider a cybersecurity enhancement project. But improving your data protection posture is not a one-time event. New threats emerge every day, and your defenses need to be monitored and revised over time. From now on, data security is a part of doing business.

Sensible Password Management

Password policies are good and necessary, but are we getting carried away?

By now you are probably familiar with one of the greatest risk areas in Information Security. It's Password Management, the policies and process by which user passwords are created, changed, managed, and eventually disabled.

It's well known that easy-to-guess passwords like "123456" or "MyPassword" are insecure and downright dangerous. There are standard recommendations that, if followed, will definitely make a given user's password hard to guess. But how far will you go to make the user passwords on your company network more secure; that is, harder to guess or steal? Is there a limit?

Does additional security have to be balanced with practical considerations? "No way", I can hear you saying. But let's consider the question a little more closely.

Do you perform every procedure in the way that is most secure, or do you also try to minimize effort, cost and practicality? Really?

Do you have red and blue pen-testing teams carrying out simulated cyber attacks and testing the defenses on your network on a regular basis? That's a great way to find vulnerabilities and test your readiness to protect your data. Some companies do this, but it's costly.

Do you take a full backup of all data on all your servers every day? That's the best way to make sure it's all available after an incident. Or do you save time, storage, and cost by using differential or incremental backups, even though that increases the odds that you might have trouble restoring everything?

We could go on, citing the ways in which we regularly balance cost and effort against the most secure possible procedures. It happens, and it should happen. But what about password management? Which of the common rules and guidelines make sense?

Let's first consider the cost of a network user not being able to recall her password. First, she has to stop whatever she is doing, and productivity drops to zero, at least while the guessing and frustration continue. Secondly, security drops as the password (or a new password) might soon be scribbled on a sticky note, and posted on the desk or wall for the world to see. Thirdly, now the person (in IT Support?) who is being contacted to help this user has to invest their time, which is not without cost. And there are other drawbacks to being frustrated and unproductive.

So yes, a company may seek a balance between the most extreme password management policies and the ease of remembering the password. Here are my thoughts on specific policies, which are commonly enforced in Windows itself, so they are easy to implement.

1. Password Length: 14 characters. I have no beef with that.

2. Password Complexity: Requires 3 of the 4 character types (lower, upper, numeric, special characters). OK, no problem.

3. Must change password every XX days. Don't like it. Leads to forgotten passwords.

4. Can't re-use prior passwords. Don't like it, for the same reason.

5. Minimum password age before changing: Again, don't like it.

I am a big fan of using complete words in your passwords. Which one is easier to remember, "OperationElbow42" or "v2wAq#^9u0Hh1r"? Both meet the 3-out-of-4 character types guideline (lower case, upper case, number, special character). All good there. But the latter one does not exactly lend itself to being memorized.

And imagine having to change every month and not being allowed to re-use an old password? You can see how passwords get written on sticky notes. If your users are outside customers rather than employees, can your relationship survive their annoyance?

How about two-factor authentication? I'm OK with obscure questions and answers, but be careful with the tactic of sending an SMS message to a mobile phone. If you travel and use different mobile phones in different countries, or if you ever change cell phones, the code-by-text technique is a nightmare.

In general, I don't like 2FA, and I am one of the few people who feels that way. I just think it places too much reliance on the mobile device and how it's used. 2FA using email as the additional factor is a little bit better, although a password and an email address and additional password may not be considered to be separate factors. Both fall under the "something you know" category.

And there are entire books available that cover how to hack 2FA (or MFA, with multiple factors) so it's not ironclad at all. But there are still many online services that force it onto you, with no other option, which I really resent as a customer. Again, many experts disagree.

Finally, I know there are password management systems that will generate remember your passwords for you. But are they without effort and cost, and are they 100% reliable? And would you need to have the entire organization utilize one to handle the most extreme password rules?

Beyond that I don't like the idea of having a password created for me, and then forced on me. When I sign up for an online service of some type and the enrollment process concludes with "Here is your new password" I become annoyed immediately. That password MIUST be written down, either in a notebook, in an email, or on the venerable post-it note. If you are in a position to make security policy, PLEASE don't force passwords on your users.

Remember, these are my views, and you don't need to call me if your password gets stolen someday. But someone has to say it: Consider your users before you automatically jump on to the most severe restrictions or methods. A system that an authorized user cannot access due to extreme security measures is not providing very good utility.

Give Me One Security Measure

Recently I was chatting with a manager at a small company about information security and the dangers we all face. She was annoyed with what she had read in the security blogs and online articles. In her opinion, she faced the choice of doing nothing at all to defend her company's data, or buying into a complex web of new technology, altered procedures, and ongoing expense.

So she challenged me, as a certified cybersecurity professional to tell her just ONE STEP she could take that would make her company incrementally safer. Just one measure, with some amount of benefit, no matter how small.

I refused. Life is not always that simple. But she did haggle me down to two, so I began thinking of TWO simple steps she could take that would let her sleep a little easier at night. Yes, they are both very simple, and require no technical or security expertise.

Good-bye to 123456

The first step is to review the way that users create passwords, and to educate everyone with access to any device, on or off the network, on password guidance. You can even keep it super-simple and say that all passwords should be changed today, and each user should set their network (and other devices) password to a value made up of two words and 2 numbers. Like maybe "happysneaker47".

Yes, it's even better to make sure you have capital letters and small letters and numbers, and maybe even special characters. But the rule-of-thumb is that it should be simple enough that everyone can remember their password(s), without writing them down. Avoid monster passwords like "a6W@3dPj7" unless you have a photographic memory.

Yes that's a few things, I suppose. But it is no longer recommended that passwords be regularly changed, which results in chaos. And I did not mention a suggested length of 12 or more. So, let's call that Step One and move on.

Backups

Yes, Step Two is plain old data backups. This may be a boring topic until the day you fall victim to a ransomware attack. Your computer is essentially dead. Now it becomes really interesting, as the hapless victim starts digging around, trying to find the most recent backup copy of some very important files or documents.

It turns out that for Windows computers, it's pretty easy to activate and schedule automated backups. It should be just about as easy to take a peek at the "destination" of your backups, to see that they are actually being recorded. You can do your backups manually if you like, as long as you remember to do them regularly.

Make sure you back up your data to another device, rather than copying files to a different location on the same computer. When a backup resides on the same drive, or even the same computer, as the original file(s), they may all disappear together.

If I might add one more suggestion, you can enhance your security if you make sure your most critical data is stored on a server (rather than a user's desktop) somewhere on the network. That allows you to concentrate your back efforts on one single server machine, or a few servers. Still, backing up user workstations is important as well. But keeping the "crown jewels" (a customer list? written contracts? the formula for Coke?) in one place will be reassuring.

Feeling ambitious? It's a fantastic exercise to create a data asset inventory. For EACH data store in your business, write down where it lives, how you are protecting it, where it's backed up, and what would happen if you lost it. This data inventory should be consistent with your backup procedures, but you may be surprised. See the Information Security Policy template in an earlier chapter for a sample asset inventory form..

Ok, that's several tips again. But it's really one defensive measure, which we can call "Data Backups".

You probably noticed that these steps don't cost anything to implement, just a small amount of time. In fact, there are many free steps and techniques you can utilize to make your data and systems more secure. I always suggest that these are the first steps you should take.

Cybersecurity Business and Cyber War

The world of information security, data breaches, and cyber attacks is still growing, both in the variety of threats and the amount of time and money being expended. There are still lone hackers and corporate misfits causing damage to private individuals and corporate entities. For example, stealing credit card numbers and login and password combination for sale on the dark web. And there are large and small cybersecurity consultants and software developers earning a living keeping cyber risks at bay.

Yet, two very different cybersecurity universes exist that may overlap, but are distinctly different in fundamental ways. No, it's not Microsoft vs Linux. And it's not red teams against blue teams.

Let's think about "private hacking" and compare it with the efforts and growing capabilities of nation states which are largely the work of what are termed "cyber warriors". Of course, business and personal data breaches are not trivial, and can be very expensive to try and recover from.

However, the advances in nation-on-nation cyber warfare (and that's what it is) tell us that this is where the real news is. An honest assessment of the ongoing offensive activity by Russia and China, and occasionally by the US and its allies, leads to one conclusion: We are at cyber war with both of our global rivals (at least), and we have been for a long time.

The massive cyber attack executed by Russia in 2020 and their election meddling in 2016 (and other events) demonstrate that these folks are investing heavily in information warfare and cyber offense. They tend to utilize non-government hacking groups, kind of like an online Russian mafia. But there is no question that the Russian government is directing and encouraging their work. This is happening now, today, and will be happening tomorrow as well.

And China, although considered somewhat less capable than Russia, has copied massive amounts of data from defense and industrial networks and servers. China has openly embraced the doctrine of "attack first to weaken the enemy" in preparation for a possible conflict with the US, or its allies in Taiwan.

And it is widely suspected that China has planted "logic bombs" inside the networks that control the US power grids and other utilities. These critical systems go by the acronym "SCADA". The nasty pieces of malicious code can be activated at any time to bring down the whole SCADA network and cripple the US economy. Keep in mind that I am writing from the perspective of an ordinary American.

Yes, this is serious stuff.

What Can We Defend?

Each US military branch (especially the Air Force and Navy) has cyber capabilities, both offensive and defensive. We have a variety of defenses in place, and the capacity to launch attacks too. And the NSA (National Security Agency) and US Cyber Command are very large organizations of capable officers and cyber warriors. So, we are certainly not asleep at the wheel. But what are we truly capable of defending? Certainly not everything that needs defending.

Richard Clarke's book *Cyber War* is more than ten years old now. But it still has a lot to teach us about where we are headed. I recommend it heartily.

On that note, I will leave you with a few questions:

If another country dropped a traditional bomb on IBM, Microsoft or Solar Winds within the US, we would expect a military response. So, when a cyber attack is visited on these companies, should our national defenses (NSA, Cyber Command, or other) be used to respond? Remember, these are private corporate assets and systems we are talking about.

Should the US government or military spend time defending your personal information? How does your private photo album or social media activity compare with securing the nation's power grid and transportation systems? Where is the priority?

Traditional "kinetic" wars are, at least in theory, governed by a set of international agreements that supposedly limit the horrors of war. (This is debatable.) Hence the term "war crimes". Will the international community ever come to a consensus and establish laws that limit cyber attacks and identify certain actions that must not be performed? What kinds of hacks or malicious code should be prohibited by international agreement?

I will answer only the last question here: It's not going to happen, at least not anytime soon.

Planning For a Little Failure

Be prepared for a successful cyber attack or data breach and you just may survive it.

Ransomware attacks are back in the news, as big-time hackers are successfully attacking big companies and national infrastructure. Some victims are paying the ransom, and many have Cyber Insurance to help defray the costs. These is no doubt – learning that you are the victim of one of these attacks is no fun. And many smaller companies, nonprofits, and government are departments are finding this out the hard way.

Let's all agree to spend whatever money and personnel resources it takes to be certain that we will never fall victim to ransomware or any other cyber attacks. We are going to be perfect and absolute in our cyber defenses.

Or is this the only option? What about resiliency? What about acknowledging that we may well be successfully attacked in some way, at some point, and we will just have to deal with it. And this is even more likely now that many workers are splitting work time between home and office. So please bear with me.

Turning our attention specifically to ransomware, let's review the common-sense steps that should be taken to reduce the odds, and more importantly the damage, of a ransomware attack:

1. Keep your most critical data on a server, not a single user's desktop computer.

2. Make sure your computer is running the latest version of its operating system (Is anyone still running Windows 7?)

3. Turn on the Auto Updates feature on your computer to ensure the latest security patches are in place.

4. Set up automatic backups for your computer (onto another computer or server, of course).

These steps are not rocket-science, but they certainly reduce the threat. And only #2 and #3 reduce the **odds** of an attack, the others reduce the **damage**. In a sense this acknowledges that no matter what we do, we may someday walk into our workplace and see the dread ransomware "Gotcha" message on our computer display.

There is one other tactic I use to protect critical documents or code that I have spent a lot of time creating. I email the file(s) to myself via Gmail. Now I know that no matter happens there is a copy of the document out there in the cloud with my Gmail archives. Google Docs works well for this too. It's an amateur tactic, but I'm not proud.

A few years ago I let my work computer get behind on its updates and, sure enough, I was hit with a ransomware attack. I responded by executing the following brilliantly conceived plan:

1. I stared at my computer screen for 10 minutes in disbelief.

2. I used my laptop to research what a Bitcoin is and what it was worth.

3. I unplugged my computer/paperweight and placed it in the corner of my office.

4. I went to the store and bought an inexpensive desktop computer.

There was software to install and a few things to set up, but I was back on my feet in a day, about $1000 poorer, and hopefully a little wiser. I had backed up (or emailed) just about everything I needed for several months, and so no tears were shed. You can survive an attack with minimal damage if you are prepared.

Keeping my operating system up to date would have been another way to be prepared, as would a formal, automated backup scheme.

Do You Really Need a Formal Information Security Policy?

Most small companies can still remember when they first launched, and they had to put together a formal Business Plan. It included forecasts (often optimistic) and projections of future operations and profits. The bank needed to see this Business Plan in order to provide funding.

Fast forward a few years and most small company CEOs are willing to admit that their initial business plan was either wildly inaccurate and/or is now collecting dust on a shelf. This document was often really only used to get financing, after which its useful life was over.

Now days most companies have prepared what is known as an Information Security Policy. Let's hope these important security frameworks are treated as "living documents" and are not relegated to the archives or file cabinet.

Purpose of an Information Security Policy Document

The purpose of a formal Information Security Policy (ISP) is to provide a framework of guidelines, procedures, rules and defensive measures for the protection of company and customer information assets.

Its goal is to reduce the chances of a data breach, system hack, or privacy violation by mandating better practices, processes, and monitoring, and requiring user education. Adopting these policies demonstrates to customers, employees and stakeholders that the company takes data security and privacy seriously. It provides a road map of how behaviors and technology are used as added security measures.

It should also provide a high-level view (at least) of common threats and defensive measures, and the steps needed to better control risk. It strongly encourages the designation of specific staff or management to be responsible for certain tasks.

This policy document is considered effective when signed and dated by management, and may be revised, reviewed, and signed off on periodically in the future. This policy document should be updated at least quarterly, to ensure that the information is current. Verify that the correct individuals are properly assigned to each responsibility, and that the responsibilities are being carried out.

Key Features

Several companies and websites will provide you with a sample ISP which can serve as a template for your final, custom data security foundation. You will likely customize it as you go, but it should have the basics already.

If you remember nothing else, here are just a few features which should really be in every ISP, no matter the industry or the size of the company or government body:

1. A signoff for management. Everyone in the enterprise must understand that the ISP is important, and that it is backed by top management. Otherwise, the whole thing is just an exercise.
2. A designation of responsibility for each sub-policy in the ISP. For example, data backup strategy and

execution could be assigned to Bob Smith, whose name will reside, in plain sight, inside the approved ISP for all to see. We all know what happens to activities and procedures that are not assigned to a specific individual.

3. The content of the ISP may include password policies, account management rules, firewall designations, wireless policies, user training, and many other sections. But the user training, often called "SAT" (Security Awareness Training") stands above every other component in a solid security foundation. Without it, all the other rules and technical measures are doomed to fail.

If you have not learned by now that the biggest data security threat you face is from your own users, you may have to learn the hard way. Training your users - managers and staff - on a regular basis offers the most "bang for the buck" as well. Also, in the ISP you need a way to keep track of what you are doing, what measures and controls have been adopted, and how well they are working.

Cyber security can be very complex (and expensive) and could be perceived by non-technical staff as a matter for the IT folks to handle. But the simple steps that management can take can have a profound impact on your risks and vulnerabilities, and they can be inexpensive to implement. That's why the "Five Easiest Steps" and the "Seven Best Practices" are available for download at flex-protection.com as well.

Whatever your operational challenges are, you can avoid an attack and cut the risks of a data breach by having a sound ISP, supported strongly by management, and updated regularly.

A Bullet-point Briefing: ISO 27001

The following highly simplified briefing will not make you an expert on the ISO 27001 requirements and documentation. And it does not replace formal training or professional services in that area. But it should help you decide if you want to embark on a project to obtain this well-known certification.

1) What is it? ISO 27001 is a global standard which specifies the implementation of policies, procedures, and controls which constitute an Information Security Management System (ISMS).

2) ISO 27001 is intended to evaluate and validate your ISMS. Your ISMS is not a software package, but essentially a collection of procedures, requirements, and controls, and lots of documentation.

3) The ISMS is designed to protect an organization's operating and financial data wherever it resides (including interfaces and databases controlled by business partners and third parties). It is very much a part of the cybersecurity world.

4) Pursuing an ISO 27001 certification for your company will add work, cost, and certainly new/revised documentation. There is no denying it. HOWEVER, you can decide on the scope of your certification; it need not cover all your operations, locations, and products/services. You can specify a reduced scope.

5)   Who needs ISO 27001? Larger companies and organizations, certainly, but also those whose customers require it. Over time, your needs may change.

6)   You need to establish a Governing Body. This is a fancy way of saying that someone from your top management team, and perhaps several executives, needs to be involved in the project, in a visible way.

7)   The ISO 27001 standard has the formal name of "ISO/IEC 27001:2013", and includes components such as ISO 27002, and others. ISO 27002, also known as "Annex A", refers to the actual documents and tools implemented in the ISMS, while "ISO 27001" refers to the standard itself. That's an important distinction.

8)   A successful ISMS achieves three objectives for your critical data, known as the CIA triad. The objectives are Confidentiality (authorized users only), Integrity (not altered or damaged, and Availability (ready when needed). It does not matter if the data is on paper, in the cloud, on your network, or on portable devices.

9)   ISO 27001 enhances information security and helps organize and validate your processes and procedures. But, if I can be slightly cynical, its real purpose may be as a marketing tool. Having the certification is considered a recognized achievement and thus allows you to advertise your compliance, which therefore creates a business advantage.

10) ISO 27001 is technology and vendor neutral and fits all industries and organizations of any size. Its cornerstone is an Information Security Policy, which you will create, and which lays the foundation for the policies, procedures and controls that follow in your ISMS.

11) The cost and duration of a certification initiative varies widely based on company size, operational complexity, and other factors. It is NOT an IT project – you can expect to allocate resources – people and time – from multiple departments and top management.

12) Implementation generally follows a simple outline, referred to as "PDCA" or Plan, Do, Check, and Act. Planning is key, and is followed by implementation, monitoring the ISMS, and acting to make corrections. It should be an iterative process (not a one-time project), with regular improvements.

13) Annex A (or ISO/IEC 27002:2013) contains the actual "controls" (114 of them, divided into 14 "domains"). You will need to become familiar with these lists – controls and domains - early in the process. It is not included here.

14) Within Annex A, you do not need to utilize every control and every document. You may choose which tools and documents you want to include. However, you are expected to create a "Statement of Applicability" that describes why certain controls were included and others were not.

15) Management support and review must be in place in order to pass a certification "audit", which is the whole point of all the additional work and expenditure.

16) Choosing controls to implement and document may be thought of as a Risk Management exercise. It is important to estimate costs, identify benefits, and choose controls based on cost/impact.

17) When addressing risk with defensive measures or operational controls, for each risk identify one of four

strategies: Avoid (change your process), Accept (hopefully only small risks), Mitigate (with defenses) or Transfer (to someone else).

18) You must conduct an Internal Audit to evaluate your ISMS. At this point you will self-verify, to reduce or eliminate surprises which may occur in the External Certification Audit to follow.

19) Your internal audit may be conducted by staff or by a third party. It will be followed by an external audit, in two stages.

20) External Audit - Stage 1: Largely a deep documentation review. You should ask your auditor in advance "What documentation will you look for?"

21) Your auditor may pause the audit after Stage 1, to allow you to make substantial corrections or improvements before proceeding to Stage 2.

22) External Audit - Stage 2: Making sure your ISMS actually conforms to ISO 27001. If successful, you can now advertise that you are "certified".

23) Non-conformities will be identified during your internal audit and possibly in your external audit. (Ex: a broken process, ignored procedures, missing documentation). You will need to address each of these (with proof of follow-up, who, when, etc.)

24) Audits are done on a 3-year cycle. In other words, to keep your certification current, you must conduct the external audit every three years.

25) ISO Service Providers / Consultants are available for projects of all sizes. You can expect to spend between $10,000 and $50,000 USD in professional services fees for support, guidance, and audits.

26) The ISO 27001 certification is considerably different from the also-popular "SOC 2" certification. You may wish to consider both options before investing in either.

27) Consider asking some of your key customers or clients what they think of ISO 27001, and whether they would find it easier to do business with you if you held this certification. The responses you get may range from 'What's that?" to "Yes, that would be impressive" and maybe even to "Yes, we require it".

Conclusion:

Expect some investment of time and money to accomplish this highly-regarded certification. It's not for everyone.

If you decide not to pursue an ISO 27001 certification at this time, that's OK. But you may wish to instead consider the following simple measures to enhance your data security:

1) Make a list of all your data stores/files, including where they live (servers, desktops, portables, home offices), expected damage if lost or breached, and how they are being protected.

2) Automate and verify your daily and weekly backups (to help you survive a successful ransomware attack). Suggest critical data be kept on servers, simplifying backups.

3) Conduct some form of User Security Awareness Training at least annually (include better awareness, latest policies, updated procedures, a security mindset, password management, safe browsing).

4) Make a list of names and phone numbers for everyone you need to contact when a security incident occurs and post the list where it can be seen. This is your bare bones "Incident Response Plan". You can certainly add more detail and instructions.

5) Consider getting some help, such as an assessment, policy review or user training from an ISO 27001 professional.

Final Note:

This ISO 27001 overview is extremely summarized, and it's STILL too long. Think about that before you bite off more than you can chew.

How Small Projects Lead to Big Projects

With enterprise software or major process changes, a small-scale pilot project usually makes sense. This view reflects the fact that I have always been "risk-averse" – I don't like risk.

Many years ago, I was a Project Manager for a large software company, much bigger than the small company I manage today. We had the size and personnel that gave us the ability to recommend a very specific methodology for implementing our enterprise software. And with millions of dollars often on the line, most customers listened.

One of my jobs was to teach our approved seven-step methodology to customers and new consultants. I also worked with a committee that oversaw the evolution and enhancement of the methodology over the years. I was fortunate to have such a role, and we had an excellent team.

Anyway, the cornerstone of the whole methodology was a crucial activity we called the "Conference Room Pilot", but commonly just referred to as a "pilot". This project phase, a project in itself, included a couple more layers of detailed tasks, but the gist of it was simple. The software was to be utilized on a smaller subset of the organization for a period of time. And this limited operation and observation generated progress reports, issue lists, ideas for future customization and so on.

The "subset" may be one division of the company, or one product line, or one geographic region. The point is that instead of perhaps 1000 users (the eventual target) the pilot would involve maybe 5-10 users, or perhaps a few dozen. The smaller scope helped manage risk, even as it yielded a highly trained group of core users who could then assist in training the broader user base afterward.

The pilot was usually run with vanilla (unmodified) software, and sometimes with manually entered test data that avoided the need for costly data conversion activity. Yes, you can enter test data (vouchers, invoices, production orders, purchase orders, etc.) much faster than you can create a trusted conversion program to accurately migrate data from one database to another. I learned that lesson the hard way.

The data items listed in the previous paragraph would correspond to the implementation of an Accounts Payable System, an Accounts Receivable system, ERP or manufacturing software, and a Purchasing / Procurement system. But the concept applies across all kinds of applications.

After years in the software business, often as a Project Manager, it seems to me that every major software implementation should be based on such a pilot. Why would there be any other approach? Lower risk, less data, clear results, problems exposed early – what's not to love?

In the realm of Learning Technology, where I have toiled for the last several years, the concept is also a good fit. Imagine that you, like one of my customers, will eventually need to service 20,000 learners with 900 online courses.

Can you identify a smaller segment of this audience, by company, location, department or product/service line? How about keeping it really simple and just starting with 3-5 online courses?

When your pilot is done, I'll bet you lunch that you will have the following in hand:

- A list of changes in how you will build online courses and tests from here.
- A list - hopefully short - of features and functions that you would like to have in the software, but have not seen yet (You may discover them later).
- A successful e-learning track record, that will generate a positive "buzz" and momentum for the larger implementation. People will spread the word.
- Experienced users and managers who are ready to move confidently ahead.

A successful pilot means momentum for a larger project.

I hear your objection: "Sure, but what if the software turns out to be a poor fit, the users are unhappy, and the pilot project is seen as a flop?" Well, in that case, you have learned the bad news quickly and at low cost, which beats the alternative.

Will your software provider be willing to arrange a smaller license for this experimental approach? They should be. I am sure they can provide some coaching as well.

And this does not just apply to training systems. As Info Security evolves and defensive technologies become more standard and commercially attractive, the exact same approach can be used. In this case, it will be normally a matter of dividing up the user community. You may also need a deeper involvement from your IT Department or Cloud Provider.

But no matter the industry or software, selecting a pilot project with a smaller scope makes financial and operational sense. And it will likely lead to the large-scale, long-term successful implementation you really want.

A Different Cybersecurity Training

Should all cybersecurity training options be aimed at users, technical staff or large companies?

A quick survey of Cybersecurity education options recently got me thinking about InfoSec education for busy Managers and Executives. Are we leaving out the real-world SMB managers and executives? Are we missing something?

I think it's like when computers were first introduced. I graduated college with a Computer Science degree and people would say "I hear you work with computers". But by the 2000's personal computers were being used everywhere and the distinction became "I am a programmer" or "I work for a computer manufacturer" or "I train users" and so on.

It's the same way now with Information Security, and Cybersecurity Training specifically. Of course, there is SAT (awareness training) that everyone in a company needs. It focuses on things like password management, cyber hygiene, phishing, physical access, good habits, etc. Very worthwhile.

And then there is more technical InfoSec training for security professionals that leads to industry-recognized certifications like Security+, CISSP, and CEH. More detailed, more concrete, than executive-level training.

And now more recently, security topics and processes that are really management-oriented have been organized into "Management Training" or "Executive Training". Is there a bias toward big corporations?

Hmmmmm. Last year I attained a CISM (Certified Information Security Manager) certification. Its focus is more on governance, planning, organization, documentation, processes, approvals, and data security concepts. It was very broad, but to boil it down it essentially focuses on the question "Can you create and manage an enterprise data security program?".

I was kicking around some ideas with a UK professional education company last year, and I took a look at a course they offered "for the boardroom". It was a special in-person course for executives (and those with a generous big-company budget!) I read through their syllabus, and it was basically identical to the CISM outline and prep materials. They were really just copying what was already out there in its totality rather than as a starting point. And it was a very short course that ran only 1 day. By my count, seventeen topics in one day. Wow!

Last year a university asked me to create and present a 15-minute introduction to Cyber Security. 15 minutes! I still have the 4-page write-up I created, and I occasionally share it with people, but you can't really do much when you don't allocate enough time. It's not really a great overview. But I learned how to summarize, and that's the point here.

What could we (InfoSec professionals) be offering as far as training for managers and executives, to help keep a small-to-medium sized company's information assets safer? Can we help reduce the changes of a successful cyber attack or data breach?

Well, if I was tasked with creating an up-to-date executive-level Information Security course, targeted at companies of ALL sizes, I would take the following approach:

1. Start with the CISM outline and information, which has good content and useful documents like a Charter, an ISP, an Asset Inventory, and several others.

2. Ask "what can we reasonably remove from the CISM outline in the name of brevity"?

3. Ask "What can we add from SAT (user training) that makes sense for executives"?

4. Ask "What can we add from the Security+ and CEH outlines that fits our mission and is not too technical"?

5. Add some ideas targeted at small and medium organizations and businesses. In my opinion, this is something that is lacking in CISM.

6. Add a section at the end of the course entitled "What you can do right now"? What are the 5 (or 10?) steps the execs can take immediately to start reducing their risk of ransomware, destructive attacks and data breaches. Yes, this is the "low hanging fruit". This take-away is the most important part of the course, in my mind.

And I would put most or all of the course online to increase access. (OK, I am biased toward online education because I am in that business - learning technology). But it could be done in person when that's practical. Or a blend, with an online follow-up to an in-person course.

Most corporate or professional training can be divided into online portions, which can be delivered asynchronously (log in at your convenience), and sections that are better off being done in person. If in-person is too expensive or impractical, then synchronous (real-time) tools like Zoom and Teams can do the job almost as well.

But one thing is certain: for managers and executives, SAT and technical training are not what's called for.

The Cost of Anonymity

Try this someday:

Take the license plate (or "auto tag") off the rear of your car and toss it in the trunk. Then go for a drive through your city or town until you eventually get pulled over. When the nice policeman approaches your window to ask you what you are doing, just tell him this: "Officer I have a right to privacy and anonymity, so I don't want to display a license plate." Let me know how that discussion goes.

We can't go out onto a road without displaying identifiable markings – our vehicle license number. But we insist on the right to engage in all manner of behavior, exploration, duplicity and mischief on the public internet (Yes, it's public) in near-total darkness.

I think this is because that's how the internet was originally designed and architected. People have gotten used to total privacy in their online world. But is it time to outgrow this idea?

I am not saying it is time to remove internet privacy, but maybe we could at least have an ongoing conversation about it. When your computer becomes useless due to a ransomware or denial-of-service (DOS) attack, it's not fun. But what's really annoying is that there is practically no way to know where it came from or who is responsible. With a pickpocket or mugger out in the physical world, at least you have a chance.

The fact is, if you have the right technical skills you can harass, block, delete, and steal information from people you will never meet. And while they can use technology to block your attack, they will never know who you are.

We all know that internet traffic travels over a standard protocol known as TCP/IP (or sometimes UDP/IP). The data is in bite-sized packets, complete with headers and footers that make sure each packet goes to the right place and is properly re-assembled. (Wow – that was concise!)

Imagine that every packet might carry an identifying number, or more than one, that indicated exactly who was responsible for creating and sending it. And without this information, no router would pass the packet on to the next router, computer or network. It would go nowhere.

Is this my technical solution for the universe of cyber attacks, and the end of hacking once and for all? Not likely. But where is the conversation about possible changes that we could be making?

Cyber security software and services are becoming multi-billion-dollar industries. Can we at least acknowledge that we are paying a high price for the privacy of a few bad actors?

There is a lot of technology in operation around the internet that keeps track or "malicious websites" and heavy email spammers. The bad guys make constant changes to avoid these tactics, but let's assume they do some good. Why can't similar technology be used to catalog the sources of harmful or clandestine traffic? Maybe we should be whitelisting (defining what gets to pass through) instead of blacklisting (using a constantly changing list of offending IP numbers and hosts). Would you be willing to label all your internet traffic with your actual name and other identifying info in order to have better security across the internet globally?

Do you feel like there is no such a thing as too much security? I am pretty sure there are differences of opinion on these matters. And there should be. I also expect that I am in the minority for even daring to suggest that universal changes to identifying users, filtering traffic, and implementing privacy rules could be made.

I recently had to prove who I was to an organization I belong to. This organization, like many others, sometimes works with law enforcement but is not an actual law enforcement agency. Their validation procedure – verifying my identity – was pretty thorough.

They used a process that required my involvement. It included validating my email address, validating my mobile number, receiving and examining my driver's license (or passport) and taking a live picture of me in real time (should have combed my hair, but I didn't know what was coming). I am pretty sure they know who I am now! The whole process took about 15 minutes and just required a cell phone with a web browser like Safari or Chrome on it. There were no snags on that day, but with all those tactics, there could have been. I wasn't given a choice.

I am just saying that we are paying a high price for the privacy of our fellow internet users, and there are ways to manage the situation. Let's start the conversation!

Made in the USA
Columbia, SC
29 July 2024

39652143R00088